Yesterday

Yesterday

| MY STORY |

by HADASSAH ROSENSAFT

with an introduction by ELIE WIESEL

YAD VASHEM AND
THE HOLOCAUST SURVIVORS' MEMOIRS PROJECT
New York • Jerusalem

This book is published by Yad Vashem, the Holocaust Martyrs' and Heroes' Remembrance Authority, c/o American Society for Yad Vashem, 500 Fifth Avenue, 42nd floor, New York, New York 10110-4299, and P.O.B. 3477, Jerusalem 91034, Israel

www.yadvashem.org

and

The Holocaust Survivors' Memoirs Project

in association with the World Federation of Bergen-Belsen Associations, Inc.

The Holocaust Survivors' Memoirs Project, an initiative of Nobel Peace Prize laureate Elie Wiesel, was launched through a generous grant from Random House Inc., New York, New York.

Second Edition, November 2005
Originally published in 2004 by the United States Holocaust Memorial Museum, Washington, D.C.

Cover photo: Lüneburg, Germany, September 1945. *Courtesy of Imperial War Museum, London*

Library of Congress Cataloging-in-Publication Data
Rosensaft, Hadassah, 1912–1997.
    Yesterday : my story / Hadassah Rosensaft.— 2nd ed.
        p. cm.
    ISBN 0-9760739-3-5 (pbk.)
    1. Rosensaft, Hadassah, 1912–1997. 2. Jews—Poland—Sosnowiec (Katowice)—Biography. 3. Jewish women physicians—Biography. 4. Women concentration camp inmates—Biography. 5. Bergen-Belsen (Concentration camp) 6. Concentration camp inmates—Medical care. 7. Holocaust, Jewish (1939–1945)—Poland—Personal narratives. 8. Holocaust survivors—Germany. I. Title.

DS135.P63R67857 2005
940.53′18092—dc22

2005054138

ISBN: 0-9760739-3-5

Printed in the United States of America.

CONTENTS

INTRODUCTION

by Elie Wiesel

On the surface, all memoirs of Holocaust survivors resemble one another. They tell of the peaceful happiness of the *before*, the terrifying violence of the Tragedy, and then, the difficult challenges that came after. This seems to be true of the broad strokes of these narratives. Except that each person evokes his or her life and agony in his or her own unique manner, distinctive voice, with his or her own distinct emphases and silences.

This is also true, even especially true, of the book the reader now holds in his or her hands. I knew its author, Hadassah Rosensaft, well. Our families were close. I used to meet her often with her husband Yossel and their son Menachem.

Yossel, full of ideas and creative energy, had an exuberant, dynamic personality which Hadassah sometimes had to moderate. She knew how to observe and liked to listen. She watched people and saw through their masks. She listened to them and understood even what they tried to hide. That is how I remember Hadassah Rosensaft. Discreet, she spoke little. But when she took part in a discussion, one paid attention. She didn't speak up unless she had something essential to add.

Naturally, everything connected with the tragedy of European Jewry interested her. She enjoyed meeting friends of her youth in Sosnowiec, mostly survivors, and the former inmates of Belsen in particular. Testimonies and essays, historical documents and biographies, articles and poems, she would read everything related to the whirlwind of the 1940s; she read them in the languages she knew: Yiddish, Polish, French, German, and English. But of her own experiences in Birkenau and

Belsen, she rarely spoke. And reluctantly. I, for one, came to regret this. She had stories, so many stories to tell about her past.

Now, in this volume, she has opened a window into her life. It is to her granddaughter Jodi that she agreed to unburden herself, in other words, to bear witness for future generations.

Already ill, she tells Jodi, and through her, all of us, about her childhood in Poland, her studies in France, the years of anguish under German occupation, the sense of abandonment, the death of those dearest to her and the utter despair in Birkenau where the physician-assassin Josef Mengele ruled, the battle for survival and the solidarity among the prisoners at Belsen, and the liberation.

All is written in a style both sober and solemn. Certain passages are heart wrenching. The hunger, the fear, waiting for the unknown. The deportation. The last journey. The separation from her family: in the blink of an eye she was torn forever from her husband and their little boy. In a few words she conveys unspeakable suffering: "My husband was holding our little boy. We stood together, behind my parents and my sister. Suddenly, there was chaos and screaming. One SS man . . . with a single movement of his finger . . . was sending some people to the right and some to the left. Men were separated from women. People with children were sent to one side, and young people were separated from older-looking ones. . . . As we were separated, our son turned to me and asked, 'Mommy, are we going to live or die?'"

She must have been haunted by this moment all the time. How could she not have suffered from it? But no doubt out of reticence, she never refers to it again in the memoir. Other events follow. The transfers from one camp to another, the selections, the sadism of the German SS men and women, the acts of compassion and solidarity of starving and crushed inmates who remained human despite the efforts of their torturers to dehumanize them. One's heart breaks as one reads, and one stops; one says to oneself that this is the limit, that one has reached the limit of cruelty, the limit of endurance, the limit of despair, the limit of the imaginable. But in the next chapter, the next stage, one realizes that, far more than Good, Evil can be infinite, increasing in magnitude as it hurls through a bottomless pit.

But Hadassah's account does not end there. She describes life in liberated Belsen, the courage of the survivors in confronting so-called normal life, their struggle for dignity, miraculous reunions, ceremonies, weddings, the rebirth of Zionist groups, the opening of schools, the demonstrations on behalf of a Jewish State. And, of course, the encounter with Yossel. Their active life on behalf of memory in Europe and especially in America . . .

Ultimately, the reader, upon closing the book, realizes that in fact, we should thank not only the author for having written it, but also her granddaughter Jodi for having listened and for having been its inspiration.

Translated from the French by Menachem Z. Rosensaft

CHAPTER 1

My Youth

My darling Jodi. You were only four years old when you first noticed the ugly blue number on my left arm. You often touched it with your little finger, and I felt that you were trying to erase it. "Grandma Dassah," you asked, "what is this? Why do you have this number? Can't you wash it off?" I answered that many years ago, bad people had written it on my arm. I know my answer was not a good one, but how could I explain my number to a child? Therefore, now that you are old enough to understand, I have decided to write my story for you.

Once upon a time, I was a young girl, just like you. My name was Hadassah Bimko. Everybody called me "Hudzia." I was born on August 26, 1912, in Sosnowiec, which is located in the southwest part of Poland, near the German border. My parents were both Hasidim, followers of the Rebbe of Ger. My father, Hersh Leib Bimko, was born in Kielce, Poland. He was an only child. His father, Benjamin Bimko, died when my father was only five years old, and his mother, my grandmother Rivka, died before I was born, so I never knew either of those grandparents. My father's uncle Chaskel Bimko, who also lived in Kielce, paid for my father's education. When my father was 12 years old, he was sent to a yeshiva (a Jewish religious school) in Kraków. After graduation, he learned the profession of gold refining and jewelry manufacturing. In 1908, at the age of 26, he married my mother, and they settled in Sosnowiec, a relatively new town that offered them great opportunities.

My mother, Hendla Teitelbaum, was born in Jędrzejów, a town not far from Kielce. She was one of ten children—five girls and five boys—so that I was blessed with many aunts, uncles, and cousins on my mother's side, as well as grandparents.

My grandmother Beila came from a rabbinic family. Her brother, Reb Shamshe, an extraordinary man, was the rabbi of the town. During World War I, there was great hunger and a typhoid epidemic in the town. My mother told us that on the Sabbath before Passover, the rabbi told the congregation that he would be spending Passover with his family in Kielce. Therefore, he would not be at home, and they should not come to seek his advice about what foods were kosher. The truth was that he never left his house; he did not want to have to make judgments and possibly deprive people of what little food there was.

My grandfather Moshe Teitelbaum, a Hasid, was a lumber merchant who owned a sawmill in Jędrzejów. Three of his sons worked in the business with him. As a youngster, whenever I visited my grandparents, my cousins and I would climb the piles of lumber. I can still smell the scent of the wood.

When I was ten years old, my grandfather died at the age of 52, leaving my grandmother with seven unmarried children—five sons and two daughters. My father helped her by caring for the whole family. He enabled the three youngest to finish school and made sure her sons remained in the family business. Thanks to him, all the children married well.

I loved my family very much. Although many lived quite far from us, they visited often. They adored my mother, respected my father, and spoiled me with many toys, especially dolls. They never knew that I didn't care for dolls—I much preferred to play with other children. Many poor children lived in the area behind our house. I would often bring one or another of these children home to wash, feed, and play with. I once overheard my mother saying that I brought home diseases that even doctors had never heard of, but she never forbade me to do it.

My mother's four sisters and five brothers were all different. The uncle I loved most was the oldest, Uncle Chaim, called Henrik. He was handsome, educated, progressive, and a Zionist. At first he worked with my grandfather in the lumber business. Then he met and married Anna, a girl from Kielce, and moved there. Her uncle, Henrik Reisman, also owned a big lumber business, which served the entire territory between Kielce and Jędrzejów. I used to visit them and their two children, Lusia and Adam, during my summer vacations.

Uncle Henrik had a wonderful sense of humor. I remember one particular incident when I was 14 years old. One evening after dinner my aunt said to us, "Children, we are going out to visit my sister; behave yourselves and go to bed early." My aunt and uncle then kissed each other and said, "Good night." Puzzled, I asked my uncle the following day, "How come you said good night to each other before going out for the evening?" My uncle laughed and explained that on such a visit they usually played bridge, and when they were partners they often criticized each other for making mistakes. The criticisms were not always gentle, and they sometimes got so angry that they didn't speak on the way home. For that reason they said good night to each other before leaving. Maybe this is the reason I don't play bridge.

Uncle Henrik was a great Polish patriot. In 1918 he served in the Polish army under Marshal Josef Pilsudski, fighting against the Russians for Poland's independence. When World War II started, he put on his Polish officer's uniform and told his family that it was his duty to join the army. He hugged them and left. After the liberation in 1945, I searched for him with the help of the British Red Cross, hoping that he had somehow survived, but we found no trace of him. Several years later, in Israel, I met people from Kielce who had known my uncle. They told me they had met him during the war in Siberia, after he had been taken prisoner by the Russians. He died there. I broke down and cried as I suddenly realized that I didn't have a single close relative left in the entire world.

My hometown, Sosnowiec, was a relatively big city, located in an industrial area rich in coal and iron ore. Its population before World War II was 120,000. Thirty percent of its inhabitants were Jews, most of them businessmen or artisans who had played an important role in the city's development. Many Jews were employed in Jewish-owned factories that produced clothing, shoes, umbrellas, and other household goods. All but one of the coal mines were owned by French and Polish people. The exception was named GUSLI, after the three owners—Gutman, Szpiro, and Lieberman. Moshe Szpiro was an uncle of my future husband, Yossel Rosensaft. At the time of my birth, Sosnowiec was under Russian occupation; from 1914 to 1918, it was under German rule; then Poland regained its independence.

Sosnowiec had an important Jewish intelligentsia: teachers, writers, doctors, dentists, and lawyers. In addition to the many banks belonging to Poles, five banks were owned by Jews, including one, called the Gemilat-Chesed, that gave interest-free loans to small businesses and artisans, enabling them to exist and develop.

The Jewish community of Sosnowiec was very well organized and extremely charitable, helping the needy and supporting an old-age home and an orphanage. There was a Jewish hospital with many good doctors and an infirmary for the poor. We had a Jewish elementary school, a Jewish high school for girls, a Jewish business high school for boys, and several religious schools, including the Beth Yaakov School for religious girls. There were also a good Jewish library, four sports clubs for Jewish youth, and many Jewish political parties and movements, such as the general Zionists; Ha-No'ar ha-Tsioni; Gordonia; Po'alei Zion, a labor Zionist movement that was subdivided into right and left factions; the Revisionists; the religious Zionist Mizrachi; the non-Zionist, extremely observant, Agudah; and the radical socialist workers' party, the Bund.

The main synagogue had two rabbis, known as the old rabbi and the new rabbi. The community supported the synagogue, the rabbis, and the Jewish cemetery. Each of the Hasidic groups—Ger, Alexander, Radomsk, and several others—worshiped in its own *shtibl* (Yiddish for a small room). The women of the Hasidic families came to services only on the High Holy Days, and at those times the room was divided by a heavy curtain.

During my childhood we lived at 5 Modrzejowska Street, the first brick house in town. All the shops on the street except for the pharmacy were owned by Jews, and all Jewish businesses were closed on the Sabbath. My family had two apartments on the second floor. One was the place of business, where my parents had a gold refinery and sold articles and equipment for dentists. Next door were our living quarters, so that my mother, who worked in the business, could keep an eye on us children and the home.

I was the oldest child. When I was six years old, my brother, Benjamin (Yumek), was born, and my sister, Rachel (Rozka), arrived four years later. We children lived a happy and sheltered life. Our home was beautiful and full of love. The best time was always Friday night. After my mother lit the candles and my father came back from shul (the synagogue), we sat down at the table for dinner. Somehow the room looked different. It was always beautiful, but on Friday evenings you could feel a radiance, an aura enveloping the room. This time was special for the family. We youngsters never accepted invitations to go out that evening. We talked, sang, and listened to the wisdom of our beloved parents.

On Saturday mornings my father got up very early to study the Talmud. I joined him at 7 a.m. Although he was a Hasid, he was very open-minded and progressive. As I was studying the Bible at school, he listened to what I had learned and helped me with this subject. Our male neighbors used to come to our house on Saturday afternoons; they sat around drinking tea and having a snack, and discussing Torah. Once one of the neighbors who knew I was studying Hebrew asked my father how I was progressing. My dear father, instead of answering him, called me in, and the men started to ask me questions. I told them that we were reading the prophets, Amos in particular. When I was asked what I could say about Amos, I answered that Amos was the first socialist. This was what one of my teachers, a Communist, had told us. There was silence around the table. It was the last time my father showed off his daughter's learning.

Every Saturday, when my father returned from synagogue, he brought a guest for lunch, called an *oreah*, a Jewish man who was either needy or a stranger from out of town. It was also customary for the students at a local yeshiva, under the auspices of the Rabbi of Radomsk, to eat their lunch in different Jewish homes during the week. One of these students ate in our home on Fridays. Our parents told us that we could speak to the boy before or after the meal, but that we should not go into the room while he was eating. Maybe, they said, he was hungry and would be ashamed to eat a lot if he felt that we were watching him.

My father had tremendous integrity. When I was a child, he was elected to the leadership council of the Sosnowiec Jewish community, representing the Hasidic Jews, but he served only a short time. The leading candidate for the principal rabbinic position of the city, supported by the Hasidim of Sosnowiec, was a man my father considered dishonest. My father argued against his election, but the Hasidim insisted on supporting him. And so, rather than vote for a rabbi he did not and could not respect, my father resigned.

My father also introduced me to the beauty of Jewish literature. He read me stories by Shalom Aleichem, I. L. Peretz, and others. He recited and taught me poems by Chaim Nachman Bialik, the great Jewish national poet, whom he had known personally because Bialik had once taught Hebrew in a religious boys school in our town.

My mother never wore a *sheytl*, the wig traditionally worn by married Orthodox Jewish women to cover their hair. She was a very progressive person although she always kept a kosher home. She had finished a Russian high school. Polish schools were forbidden under the Russian occupation, but a group of girls, my mother included, secretly studied the Polish language and literature. She had very good manners and was sensitive to the way I expressed myself. She disliked exaltation or exaggeration. One day I told my mother about a new girl who had come to our class, adding, "She is such a decent girl." My mother looked at me and asked, "Do you know any girls who are not decent?"

When I was ten years old, I received a diary. I asked my mother to write in it, and she offered a rhyme in Polish, which when translated states, "In life you need very little—a piece of bread and love." I remember all this with tenderness and nostalgia. If there is any good in me, I know I owe it to my parents.

Many interesting and famous people came to our place of business. I once met Esther Rachel Kaminska, the first lady of the Jewish theater, who had come with her daughter, Ida, and Sigmund Turkow, Ida's husband, to buy a gold object for Turkow's birthday. After they bought an antique gold watch, they gave us tickets to their Sosnowiec performance of the play *Mirele Efros*. My parents took me along. It was my first time in the Jewish theater, and although I didn't understand much of the play, I was impressed.

I never attended a kindergarten or an elementary school because my mother was not yet working in our family business and spent a lot of time teaching me. When I was seven years old she took me to the Jewish high school for girls. I passed the tests and when the principal asked my mother for my birth certificate, she said she would bring it later. Somehow, she never got around to doing this. I was a good student and remained there, despite the fact that I was younger than most of the other students in my class.

Miss Lola Lieberman was the owner and principal of the school, and her two sisters, Bronia and Rose, were our teachers. They were assimilated Jews, and the school was open on Saturdays and closed on Sundays, but I never went to school on Saturday. In my third year there, Miss Lieberman fell ill and couldn't keep the school, so the parents bought it and hired a new director, Dr. Holden. He instituted drastic changes. The school was now closed on Saturdays and open on Sundays. The following year Dr. Paul (Faivel) Wiederman became our principal. A Zionist, he introduced the study of Hebrew as a modern language. Because our school was the only Jewish school for girls in the whole area, we competed academically with Polish schools. Eventually, our school received official Polish accreditation.

The school had 150 students, all of them Jewish. Only three of my classmates survived the Holocaust, and thanks to one of them, Genia Traiman, who went to Palestine before the war, I have some photographs, mementos from my school years. We were a very active group, not only in scholastic achievements but also in sports. We once even went to Moravská Ostrava, Czechoslovakia, to compete in running, gymnastics, discus throwing, and Ping-Pong. We formed a self-aid group and helped poor schoolchildren. Next to our school was a public school. We noticed that some children were so poor they didn't even have breakfast. During recess, we collected our breakfasts and passed them over to those children through the fence. For a few pennies we then each bought a bagel and a pickle for ourselves.

We formed discussion groups in literature, history, and even politics, but we were not allowed to join any political organizations until we were 16 years old. I then joined the Zionist youth organization, Yardenia, which was organized by our history professor, Joseph Lauder. He was a Revisionist, a follower of the right-wing Zionist leader Vladimir Ze'ev Jabotinsky, and he tried to run the group as a Revisionist organization. We didn't like his politics and left Yardenia to join Herzlia, a far more moderate, more progressive general Zionist youth group, which later became known as Ha-No'ar ha-Tsioni (Zionist Youth). Some of our teachers were also our friends. Three stand out in my memory: Dr. Paul Wiederman, our principal, who taught us Latin; Miss Regina Fiszler, Polish literature; and Dr. Joseph Kohn, general and Jewish history. They also took us mountain climbing and on excursions to industrial sites such as coal mines, salt mines, and glass factories.

We had two months of summer vacation. I used to spend one month with my parents, brother, and sister, and the other with my grandparents, who lived four hours away by train. After my grandfather Moshe Teitelbaum died, when I was ten years old, I promised my grandmother Beila that I would come to her every summer. I'm glad that I kept my promise until the outbreak of the war. My grandmother was a lovely lady. I listened for hours to her stories about our family. On Saturday mornings, I used to go with her to shul, carrying her siddur (prayer book). She died in March 1942, in her own house, in her own bed. It is terrible and tragic to say that when we got the news of her death we thanked God that she was spared being sent to Treblinka, where 45 members of my family were killed in the gas chambers.

At the age of 15½, I finished high school and was supposed to receive a baccalaureate diploma. But alas, at that time there was a law that one had to be 17½ years old to receive this diploma. I was heartbroken. I stayed home for a full year, reading and learning more, and the following year I went back to school for the last three months only and at last received my diploma. I wanted to go to university to study medicine, specializing in dental surgery, but I knew that I had no chance of being accepted by the medical faculty in Poland because I was Jewish. My parents gave me not only their permission to study in France but also their blessing. I still remember my father's prophetic words: "We are sending you off with all our love and may God watch over you. Remember, whatever times may come, you may lose all your possessions, but nobody can take away your education."

I often wondered why my parents did not tell me to behave, to be a good student, to remain religious, and to eat kosher food. When one of our neighbors, an old man named Shmuel Lampel, came to say good-bye to me, he put his hands on my head and said, "Do not forget whose daughter you are." I hope that I never betrayed their confidence in me.

With all these blessings, I left for France in October 1930 to study dentistry at the Faculty of Medicine at the University of Nancy. The dean of our faculty, Professor Rosenthal, was a French Jew. His son, Coco, taught us pathology. After the war, I learned that both of them and their families had perished in a concentration camp. The first two years we studied general medicine—pathology, anatomy, and so on—but the last two or three years were devoted exclusively to dental studies. I met many students from all over Europe and became rich in friends. My roommate, Hela Weinberg, was from Będzin, Poland, a town near my own. I saw her for the last time in Birkenau, where she died in December 1943.

My other close friends were Polish, too, Rela Pfeffer and Fania Ginsberg, both from Łódź, and Maurice (Mundek) Frey and Hersch Miller from Rzeszów. We studied and ate together. I ate kosher food, first because I felt that it was my kind of food, and second, because my parents had never told me how to behave or what to do; I felt that I owed them something ethically and morally so that when I returned I could look them in the eye. My father thought that every young person, every student, smoked. He never did, but as the owner of a business, he always kept a silver case filled with cigarettes for his customers. He probably wanted to see what his daughter would do, so when I came home for the summer after my first year in Nancy, he handed me the case. When I said, "Daddy, I don't smoke," I noticed that he was very pleased.

There was one kosher restaurant in Nancy. The owner, Elias, was not rich, but he was very charitable. Because he knew that students didn't have much money, he often gave us food without accepting money for it. In addition, my parents sent me food packages containing cakes, cookies, sausages, and other good things. These were welcomed and enjoyed by my friends, with whom I shared these treats.

Nancy was a beautiful city, like a small Paris. We used to get up at 5 a.m. and go to a lovely park in the Rue de la Pepinière, across from our living quarters, and sit on a bench to study. We all joined the Jewish students Zionist Organization. We often discussed the current political situation and the rise of Hitler. When he came to power in 1933, all the students at Nancy's universities protested against the rise of Nazism. At our meetings, we read the newspapers from Palestine, which was under British mandate. The British policy was rather pro-Arab and not at all favorable toward the Jews, who were not allowed to immigrate freely to Palestine. There were hostile encounters, sometimes even bloody confrontations, between the British and the Jews.

We did not live in the dormitory of the university but in an apartment house for students only. Our next-door neighbor, Robert, was a Spanish Catholic student of agriculture. One Sunday morning, he knocked at our door. When we opened it, he told us that he was not feeling well and asked if we could make him some tea and buy some food. This we did for several days. When he got well, he sent us flowers and chocolates. Later, we learned that he belonged to the Spanish nobility and was very rich. When we received a letter from his mother, thanking the "two Samaritan sisters" for taking care of her son, we laughed. But one evening, while we were having a meeting of our Zionist students group, Robert again knocked at our door and asked if he could come in. Hela and I didn't want to be rude, so we let him in. Our discussion was about the situation in Palestine and the physical confrontations between the British and the Jews. We were stunned when Robert defended the anti-Jewish British and insulted the Jews. I forgot my manners and told him to leave our room. For many days after this incident, he sent us flowers and letters, asking to meet with us. He could not understand why we were angry with him. We decided to give him a chance to explain his behavior. We met with him and asked him why he disliked Jews so much. Had he ever suffered at the hands of Jews? He looked at us in bewilderment, saying that he had never met any Jews, but had learned all about them at home. I asked him if he was sure about this and then told him to write to his mother that the "two Samaritan sisters" were Jewish. He was speechless and ashamed. He apologized to our student organization, became a "non-Jewish friend," and supported the organization financially. As for myself, I was very sad to realize that antisemitism is a terrible disease that does not even require the presence of Jews.

Our relationship with the French Jewish students was awkward. At the university we talked with one another cordially, but we never became friends. Those who lived in Nancy never invited any of us to visit them. One episode was particularly unpleasant, and I still find it difficult to talk about. During our first year we wanted to make a seder on Passover. We needed some provisions, such as matzos and wine, so we went to the rabbi and asked him to help us prepare a seder that all Jewish students could attend. He said that he couldn't help us because *"Je suis français d'abord, ensuite sémite"* (I am a Frenchman first and then a Jew). It was a shocking answer!

The only French Jews I got to know well in Nancy were the two sons of my parents' friends, a family named Rosen. From time to time I was invited to their home on a Friday or Saturday night. They were terribly French. One of them, who was about my age, refused to speak a word to me in either Polish or Yiddish. He was such a snob that I said to him, "Leon, if you behave like that, I don't want to know you." The other son, Adolph, was a very handsome blond man who really looked German. He worked and lived in Leipzig, but when Hitler came to power, Adolph came to Nancy to join his family. He wanted to go back to Leipzig, which is almost halfway between Nancy and Sosnowiec, and suggested that I go with him on my way home. I had never been in Germany, but foolishly went along with his idea. We traveled there by train but stayed for only a few hours. In the Jewish quarter I saw a Jewish woman with a boy. Because Adolph had a copy of a German newspaper in his pocket, the boy said to his mother, *"Mutti, da kommt ein Deutscher"* (Mommy, here comes a German). I said to Adolph, "I beg of you, let's leave here because I can't take it. I can't take their pain, their fear, and my dismay. I do not belong here. We should not have come. Bring me to the station; I want to go home." The next time I came to Germany, I was brought there without tickets.

We studied hard, but during our winter vacations, Mundek, Hersch, Hela, and I used to go to Paris to sit in on some courses at the Sorbonne and visit the city. I have loved Paris ever since. We always stayed at the home of a certain Rabbi Leibert, a distant cousin of my father. After the war, I found out that he, his wife, and their two children had been deported by the Germans and had never returned.

We always looked forward to our summer vacations. Each time we returned to Poland we took a different route and visited different countries. One year we went to Vienna, where my cousin Alter Fuerstenberg was studying with Professor Sigmund Freud, and he showed us around. Another time, we went to Basel, Switzerland, for a few hours because I, as a Zionist, wanted to see where Theodor Herzl had convened the first Zionist Congress in 1897. We also visited Prague, Czechoslovakia, where I recalled a story that my history professor, Dr. Joseph Kohn, had told us. At the beginning of the eighteenth century, the Duke of Bohemia decided to expel all the Jews. The rabbi and the elders went to plead with him. Finally, the duke agreed to let the Jews stay, but only on condition that they make a statue of black marble. On top of the statue, they had to put the figure of Christ made of golden wire and, in golden letters, I.N.R.I.—meaning *Iesus Nazarenus Rex Iudaeorum*. On the base of the statue they were to place a second inscription, also in golden letters, but this time in Hebrew: *Kadosh, Kadosh, Kadosh Adonoy Tzevaot* (Holy, holy, holy is the Lord God of Hosts). This monument had to be placed at the end of the Charles Bridge, where gray stone statues of the Apostles stood. The rabbi agreed to these demands. The elders were shocked, but the rabbi told them it was only a piece of stone. "We Jews don't believe in statues, and Jewish life is more precious than gold and stone."

I had always thought this story was a myth, but being in Prague, I could not re-sist exploring the truth. My friends and I went to the bridge and found and counted the gray sculptures of the apostles and saints. Then, at the very end of the bridge, we saw a shining black marble statue, exactly as my teacher had described. The statue with its Hebrew inscription is still there. I saw it again in 1987.

My summer vacations lasted three months. I was happy to be home, surrounded by my loved ones, seeing my parents. My brother and my sister were growing up, and I was pleased that they were nice youngsters, getting a good education. I enjoyed seeing my school friends, especially Josef Prejzerowicz, the son of our neighbors and the heartthrob of my teens. He was six years older than I. My mother noticed that he was in love with me, but she thought that I was not aware of it. She used to tell me that Josef was coming to read the newspapers, as my parents subscribed to Polish, Yiddish, and Hebrew papers. In later years, we used to laugh about it.

I also visited my grandmother and enjoyed every day of my time with her. The return to Nancy was always difficult.

I was in Nancy for four and a half years. I finished my studies in June 1935, receiving the degree of *Chirurgien Dentiste* (Surgeon Dentist) with honors. Then I returned home. My brother, Yumek, was finishing high school and hoped to go to Palestine to study at the Hebrew University in Jerusalem. My sister, Rozka, was only 13 years old. She was very gifted and hoped one day to go to Vienna to study arts and crafts.

After a little rest, I sent my diploma to Warsaw for registration and accreditation and started to work. Thanks to my parents' business connections, I got a very good position in a dental clinic under the municipal social services administration, where I worked until the beginning of the war. On March 14, 1936, I married Josef. He was then the director of a lumber mill. On December 3, 1937, our son Benjamin (Beni) was born. He was a sunny little boy, blond, with big blue eyes. He filled our hearts with joy. We were happy, well-off, and looked forward to a happy future.

CHAPTER 2

The Beginning of the War Years

During the years before the outbreak of World War II, antisemitism in Poland took on new forms. Jewish students at universities were harassed, molested, forced to stand during the lectures. Economic boycotts against Jewish businesses began. Young Polish men stood outside Jewish stores, picketing and holding posters that read, "Poles. This is a Jewish shop. Do not buy here!" There were even pogroms, one in the little town of Przytyk, where many Jews were killed. The Catholic Church made no effort to help us; on the contrary, some priests spoke openly against Jews. The Polish people did not react either. The news from Germany was frightening. Instead of realizing that Hitler was our common, dangerous enemy and that united action against Germany was called for, the Poles were against us Jews.

We lived in ever-growing fear, listening to and reading about what was going on in Germany. In October 1938, the Germans sent about 17,000 Jews to Poland; these were Jews who were originally from Poland, many of whose families had lived in Germany for years, even generations. For many weeks the Polish government refused to admit these Jews, who were held in a no-man's-land either near Zbąszyń in northwest Poland or in Beuten, Upper Silesia, in southwest Poland, not far from our town. All the Jewish organizations tried to help ease the suffering of the stranded Jews. Young people, among them my brother, helped by guarding the borders day and night and providing food and other necessities. Even non-Jewish Polish restaurant owners in our area helped feed them. Poland finally agreed to let them in. They told us terrible stories about what was going on in Germany. In spite of this, very few Jews left Poland.

I recall two letters from Menachem Ussishkin, president of the Jewish National Fund, the Keren Kayemet, in Palestine. One was written to the Zionist youth organization, Ha-No'ar ha-Tsioni, thanking them for the gift of a small silver Keren Kayemet box made by my brother. The other letter was to Yumek, inviting him to come to Palestine. My parents and I begged him to go, but he felt that as the only son, he had no right to leave us just to save himself. These were the morals and ethics of Jewish families like ours, and that is why the tragedy and the losses were so great. I often think that if Yumek had gone to Palestine, I would still have had my brother now.

By August 1939, we realized that war was inevitable. Poland expected a German invasion. There were appeals over the radio, urging mothers with small children to move away from areas near the German borders. I went with my baby, who was not even two years old, to Jędrzejów, to stay with my grandmother and uncles. My husband and the rest of the family were supposed to join me but were never able to do so because the situation turned into complete chaos. People were fleeing from one place to another, hoping to escape the Germans. Unfortunately, all these attempts were futile. The Germans invaded Poland on September 1, 1939; their victory was immediate and complete. Ironically, they came to Jędrzejów first. I found myself stranded, far away from my dearest ones in Sosnowiec. I was desperate. How would I get back? There were no trains running, and there were rumors that the Germans were killing people on the roads. Rosh Hashanah and Yom Kippur went by, and I was still cut off from my family.

One day I was walking in the street, unaware that tears were running down my face. Suddenly I heard a voice: "Miss Bimko, why are you crying?" I looked up and saw the coachman, Moishe, who always drove passengers from the railroad station into town, including, naturally, members of our family. I explained my desperate situation to him, saying, "Moishe, how can I ever get home?" Without hesitation, he said, "Stop crying, please. I will take you and the baby home." I told him that it was a noble gesture, but I could not accept his offer because it would be a very dangerous journey. I vividly remember his reply: "When my father died, my mother was left with six children, all boys. We were very poor, and your grandfather, Moshe Teitelbaum, took care of us. He provided food, clothing, and sent us boys to the *heder.* He cared for us until we were able to work. I never had the opportunity to repay this debt or to show my gratitude. Now you must let me do it."

I argued with him but to no avail. He went to my uncle and told him that he would put on peasants' clothes, that he knew all the roads through Polish villages where he had Polish friends. He assured my uncle that he would bring us home safely. My family had heard rumors that there was a lack of food in the area of my hometown, so they loaded the coach with food, and we left. Our journey lasted three days and two nights, although it would have taken only four hours by train. We had to stop early in the evenings because of curfew. We slept in Polish peasants' huts, and finally Moishe brought us home safely. You can imagine how happy my family was to see us. They greeted Moishe with open arms and kept him with us for two more days to let him get some rest.

After my return, I found that many Jews had already been killed, others imprisoned. The synagogue had been burned down and Jewish stores confiscated. A Jewish council, called the Judenrat, was established on German orders. The head of the council was Moniek Merin, a brother of my classmate Rose Merin. The orders stipulated that the Judenrat would be fully responsible for the implementation of German policy regarding the Jews and would be made up of influential members of Sosnowiec's Jewish community. The Germans took over important Jewish businesses and assigned each one to a trustee, or *Treuhänder.* While awaiting the appointment of such a trustee for my parents' business, something unusual happened. During World War I, two sisters had come from Latvia to our town. Both Dr. Anna Weiss, a pediatrician, and Dr. Nadyezda Weiss, a dental surgeon, were single and of the Greek Orthodox faith. Dr. Anna worked in the local Jewish hospital, and Dr. Nadyezda opened a private practice. Being a dentist, she became a customer of my parents and a friend as well. When she learned that a German trustee was to be appointed for our business, she went to the Gestapo without saying anything to my parents and registered as a *Volksdeutsche,* although she was an ardent anti-Nazi. She asked specifically to be assigned as a *Treuhänder* for our business. When she made an inventory for the Germans, she listed only half the goods, which enabled us to sell the rest. She never used the salary she got from the Germans but gave it to my father, who in turn gave it away to needy Jews.

Because I lived on Pieracka Street in an area that was forbidden to Jews, I had to move to my parents' home, where I opened my dental practice. A partial ghetto was soon established. We did not have to move because our street became part of the ghetto, but our movements were restricted. Some streets were off-limits for Jews; on others, Jews were allowed to walk on one side only. We could use the trolley, but we had to stand outside, on the platform. Jewish doctors and dentists were forbidden to treat non-Jewish patients, although there were some Polish doctors in the ghetto. One of them—I forget his name—tried to help save little boys, aged four or five, from the threat of death by attempting to conceal their circumcisions. I don't know how he did it, but somehow, in his office, he applied special surgery to their foreskins. Then they could be given to Polish families for hiding. If he had been caught, he would have been killed. Many Poles, however, were very happy about what was happening to the Jews.

We had to put our names on a blue plaque with a yellow star and affix it to the outside of the house. Men had to add the name "Israel" to their first names, and women, "Sarah." We were forced to wear a white armband with a blue Star of David in the middle.

On October 26, 1939, after the Germans had occupied Poland, they established an administrative unit, the General Government, with its center in Kraków. Later, they incorporated Łódź and our area into the German Reich. This area was then called East Upper Silesia. From that time on, we had to affix a yellow star with the word *Jude* in the center to the left side of our clothing.

Other edicts were then issued. A curfew was declared. Through the Judenrat, we had to deliver all radios, gold, silver, and furs to the Germans. Jewish schools were closed, and Jewish children were forbidden to attend Polish schools. Still, youngsters formed groups and tried to study. Two sisters, Renia and Fela Zimmerman, organized a kindergarten in their apartment, where small children, mine included, spent a few hours playing every day. It was a welcome relief for many working mothers.

Our situation worsened every day, and life became increasingly difficult. We lived in constant danger. The very important issue was work. I was working in the hospital. During the winter of 1939–1940, every Jew up to age 55 was ordered to work seven days a month in places determined by the Judenrat. Mostly they were told to sweep the streets and pick up the garbage. Wealthy Jews were able to avoid this kind of work by paying bribes to members of the Judenrat.

On the eve of Rosh Hashanah in 1940, two Gestapo men came to our apartment, looked around, and stopped in my parents' bedroom. They confiscated the furniture of the bedroom—beds, night tables, an armoire, and a vanity table, all in light birch-wood. Where and how would our parents sleep? We were desperate, and then some-thing beautiful happened. Across the street lived two brothers named Baitner, who were upholsterers. They saw what happened, came to us, and said that they would make two mattresses for my parents. Even though they were very religious Jews, they didn't go to prayers on this Rosh Hashanah eve but worked until they had finished and delivered the mattresses.

We witnessed much goodness in many people. There were Jewish bakeries that distributed bread. As I never allowed my parents to go out, I went to stand in line for bread. The man who distributed the bread at the Hampel bakery near our home, Mr. Sendel, was the prewar president of the Sosnowiec Jewish community. When he spotted me, he told me not to stand in line. Every day, he brought us two loaves of bread. That bread was an important addition to the food rations we received: 200 grams of bread daily, and once a week, 100 grams of margarine, 100 grams of sugar, and 100 grams of jam. Sometimes we were able to buy a piece of fish from our janitor.

Then we had another great help. The Jewish community obtained a piece of land for gardening, which was divided into parcels and rented to some Jews. We were fortunate enough to get one of those plots. Every morning, before my own work, I went to the piece of land with my sister. We grew potatoes, beets, and onions, and as we had plenty, we shared the vegetables with our neighbors.

My classmate Rose Merin, sister of the head of the Sosnowiec Judenrat, was the supervisor of that gardening spot. She had refused to accept a position at the Juden-rat because her ethics were strong. Rose was married but had no children. When she was deported, she arrived in Birkenau together with her best friends and their little girl. During the selection at the arrival, she noticed that mothers with children were being kept on one side, to be sent to the gas chambers. Without hesitation, she grabbed her friends' child, saying, "I want to pay for my brother's sins."

Because of my brother's frequent absence, I felt it was my duty to watch over the family. I trained myself to sleep very little. Endless evenings listening to the frightening footsteps of Nazi boots were followed by sleepless nights. Each day I was more afraid than on the previous day. Yumek belonged to the underground movement, made up of the Jewish youth organizations Ha-No'ar ha-Tsioni, Ha-Shomer ha-Tsa'ir, and Gordonia, which called on the Jews to resist the edicts issued by the Germans through the Judenrat. Because my brother and his friends worked during the day, they had to meet at night. They tried to work out a way to help Jews escape the ghetto to other countries, especially Hungary, in hopes of reaching Palestine. They also heard that some Jewish young people had organized themselves into partisan groups who lived in the forests and tried to sabotage the Germans. The leader of Ha-No'ar ha-Tsioni was Josef Korzuch. In June 1942, Mordecai Anielewicz, later the commander of the Warsaw ghetto uprising, illegally visited our underground resistance groups and told them about the situation of the Jews in other parts of Poland, about the deportations and gas chambers and crematoria. After Anielewicz's departure, the groups intensified their work; they had connections with the Jewish Committee in Switzerland, especially with Saly Mayer, the Swiss Jewish leader and representative of the American Joint Distribution Committee (AJDC), which helped get Jews visas for South American countries. On one occasion, Moniek Merin and his assistant, Fanny Czarna, approached Korzuch, Yumek, and another member of the underground, Samek Meitlis. The Judenrat officials wanted to know about the Swiss connection, but my brother and his friends refused to tell them anything.

My sister, Rozka, became engaged and was married in our apartment. She and her husband, Manek Rosman, hoped to have a chance to leave Poland, but their efforts were futile. My brother-in-law, like many other young Jewish men, was sent to a labor camp, Bunzlau, and my sister remained with us. Because of the construction of a large concentration camp near the town of Oświęcim (in German, Auschwitz), the entire Polish and Jewish populations were evacuated from that area. In April 1941, just before Passover, 2,000 Jews from the town of Oświęcim and its surrounding area came to our town. The local Jewish population reacted immediately. In spite of being overcrowded ourselves, a place to live was found for every new family, and every family was welcomed at the seder table.

At the beginning of August 1942, we received news that all Jews from Kielce and the surrounding area had been sent to Treblinka and killed in the gas chambers. Among them were 45 members of our family; my aunts, uncles, and cousins were gone. Only Ida, my mother's youngest sister, who lived in Sosnowiec, was left. But Ida and her little girl, Tusia, were subsequently killed in Birkenau; her husband, Shlomo Bergman, was sent to a labor camp. He survived and lives in Israel, where I have seen him during my visits there.

Another of my father's cousins, Sarah Fuerstenberg, and her husband, Shmuel Ben Dov, also survived. They fled to the Soviet Union from Poland at the beginning of the war. After the war, they went to Israel, where I met them in 1946. Sarah's brother, Dr. Alter Fuerstenberg, whom I had visited in Vienna during my student years, was killed by the Germans. A brilliant student, Alter had received his baccalaureate from a Polish high school after finishing his yeshiva studies. He then went to Vienna to study for the rabbinate, but one of his professors told him that he should study psychiatry instead, and introduced him to Sigmund Freud. Alter studied with Professor Freud, finished with honors, and returned to Poland. It took him only six months to pass the Polish examinations at the University of Warsaw. He then opened a practice in Kielce.

When the war started, Alter, his wife, and their two-year-old son fled to Kostopol, a little town situated in that part of Poland that had been occupied by the Russians. There, he became director of a children's hospital. In 1941, after Germany had declared war on the Soviet Union and invaded the Soviet-held sector of Poland, the Germans occupied Kostopol. One day, two Gestapo men came to the hospital and demanded that Alter give them the names of the very sick Jewish children. Alter answered that he needed a few days to prepare such a list. When the Gestapo men returned after two days, Alter handed them a sheet of paper with only three names: his own, his wife's, and his son's. They were all executed by hanging.[1]

Because the Germans needed an enormous workforce as part of their war efforts, they organized a department to force the population of occupied countries to perform slave labor in factories and mines and labor camps inside Germany. The main office of this department for our area of Upper Silesia was at the Sosnowiec Judenrat. The Germans ordered the Judenrat to provide them with Jewish workers. A transit camp, called the Dulag *(Durchgangslager)* was established in the former Jewish high school. There, Jews who had been taken from their families were kept, sometimes for weeks, until they were sent to the German labor camps. If a person named on the list did not appear, the Judenrat had the ghetto's Jewish police, the Milice, take another person from that family, called an *ersatz*, by force.

Mass transports were sent to the labor camps in 1941. Moniek Merin and other

---

1. This incident is described in the *Memorial Book of Kielce* and in *Martyrdom of Jewish Physicians in Poland* (New York: Exposition Press, 1963).

members of the Judenrat appealed to the young people to go work in Germany in order to save the rest of the Jewish population of Sosnowiec and the surrounding area. Merin told them that the work would last only six weeks, but the truth is that those who went to the labor camps did not come back. Most Jews did not want to go to the labor camps. At first only poor Jews were sent. Those who were able to pay off the Judenrat remained at home. There was a great fear that if all the young Jews were sent away, the lives of the older people and children who remained behind would be in danger.

To ease the situation, the Jews in Sosnowiec came up with the idea of establishing workshops that would employ men, women, and even children over ten years old and would thus help them live, at least for a while. The German officials stationed in Sosnowiec were in favor of this idea, first because it would keep them from going to the Russian front, and second, because they could make a lot of money by accepting bribes. The first of these workshops, established by the Judenrat in 1941–42, was owned by a German from Berlin named Hans Held. Four thousand Jews found work there, producing military uniforms, lingerie, and other articles for women. A workshop called Braun produced boots for the German army; 1,400 Jews worked there. Another firm, Lande (which also operated a labor camp in Bunzlau, Germany), produced furniture for the German army and employed 600 Jews, including my husband, who was an expert in lumber. I worked in this shop's dental clinic three days a week, taking care of the workers' teeth.

In all, 13,000 Jews, almost half the Jewish population of Sosnowiec, worked in these and several other workshops. Every Jew tried to work there; special certificates, called *Sonders,* were issued as guarantees against deportation, but some small shops were liquidated in the second half of 1942 and people lost their *Sonders.*

CHAPTER 3

Deportation

The deportation of Jews from our town and the surrounding area began in 1942. In May of that year, 1,000 Jews were deported to Auschwitz, the first and largest of the concentration camps in Poland. In June 1942, 2,000 more were sent. At the beginning of August, the Judenrat told all the Jews to appear at certain assembly places on the morning of August 12 in order to receive a stamp on their identification cards that would protect them from deportation. It was a cruel trick. On August 12, a very hot day, 26,000 Jews from Sosnowiec—almost all the inhabitants of the ghetto—headed toward the sports arena, the Union. On this day, we were allowed to walk through all the streets of the town. Everybody had on his or her best clothes to make a good impression. We left early in the morning, but it took many hours until everyone arrived there.

The Union was surrounded by Gestapo men and German police with heavy machine guns, and we began to feel afraid. First, we had to register at a little table, according to our initials. After that, the police pushed us all to one side of the field; the other side was empty. At noon more tables were placed on the empty side. At each table sat a Gestapo man and an official of the Judenrat. On Gestapo orders, entire families had to approach the table. Families whose members were working in important German shops received number 1 and were free to go home. Number 2 was for young people who worked in private places. They were kept aside, to be sent eventually to labor camps. Number 3 was for families in which only a few members were working. They too were kept aside, and their fate was still to be determined. Number 4 was for old people and those without work. They were detained and their destiny was Auschwitz.

We were indeed trapped. There was terrible chaos. You could not see faces, only a mass of people. People, hungry and exhausted after so many hours, were screaming and crying. Even those like us, who were free to go, could not leave until midnight.

The selections lasted until August 18. Eight thousand Jews were deported to Auschwitz. Great sadness and mourning enveloped the remaining community. In October 1942, the Germans evacuated the Polish population, poor working people, from one of the suburbs, Szrodula Dolna, and this became our ghetto. Jews were moved there in stages. Our family and all the other Jews who lived on our street were among the last to move into the ghetto. Each family took very little, only the most-needed items, because the living conditions were terribly crowded. We, a family of seven—my parents, my husband and child, my brother and sister, and I (my sister's husband had been sent to a labor camp)—got one room and a kitchen. It was very difficult, but we were still together.

On March 10, 1943, the transfer was complete and the ghetto was closed, surrounded by German police. The Jews who worked in German shops in town were escorted by German police to work every morning and back to the ghetto every evening. Doctors and dentists received licenses, only one for three doctors. We all treated our respective patients in the same place, but during different hours. My partners were Dr. Halina Grzesz from our town and Dr. Richter, a German Jew from Breslau, who had come to Sosnowiec shortly before the war. One day he received a letter from the Gestapo informing him that his house in Breslau had been sold. Dr. Richter was, unfortunately, very naive. He went to the Gestapo and complained that his house had been sold too cheaply. He never came back; he had been sent to Auschwitz.

My office was not far from our new home. Each day, while walking to work, I passed a little square where a young man played with a group of small Jewish children, between five and eight years old. They were always singing a song: "David, King of Israel." One day, they were no longer there: no teacher, no children, and no song.

I lived in constant fear. When returning from work, I always prayed that I would find everybody at home. Nobody should, God forbid, be missing, because there were often unexpected raids by the Gestapo, and thousands of Jews disappeared, most of them forever. My parents never knew of my fear because by the time I reached the door to our house, I was smiling. We still hoped that we would all survive. Many Jews started to build bunkers in the ghetto to hide in whenever they heard rumors of a raid. We had a well-camouflaged bunker in the basement, behind a kitchen wall, which we shared with two other families who lived in the same house. I never went to the bunker because I felt that I would not be able to help if I were inside—somebody had to let people in and out. At that time, I was still protected by my work permit from the Jewish hospital. During the raids, I would sit in another room, dressed in my white uniform. Before this time, I had not known what "cold sweat" meant, but I knew now.

One day in June 1943, during a raid when the Germans went from house to house taking Jews for deportation, my family and our neighbors were in the bunker. I was sitting in a room facing the stairs, pretending to read a medical book. All of a sudden, I heard footsteps. Somebody was coming down the stairs. I looked up, scared to death, and saw the tips of soldiers' boots. They were getting closer and closer. I was convinced that in seconds I would be shot or taken for deportation and my family would not even know what had happened to me. Cold sweat covered my entire body. I closed my eyes, and when I opened them I saw a man with a white hat. I could not believe it. The man was a Jewish policeman in his uniform; his mother was in the same bunker, and he had come to tell us that the raid was over. I knew that, like all the others, my family and I were living on borrowed time. We buried some jewelry and other valuables in the bunker.

Our situation became desperate. Although the news of the Allies' victories was good, we felt that we were doomed. Jews were trying to get "Aryan" papers and paid a lot of money for visas to other countries. Thanks to the American Jewish Joint Distribution Committee in Switzerland, some Jews received citizenship in South American countries, mostly Paraguay. Those Jews were placed in camps of internees. In June 1943, the German police learned that several young Jews (members of Ha-No'ar ha-Tsioni, which had acted on their behalf) had received foreign citizenship and decreed that they, too, should be sent to the camps of internees. The youngsters, 16 of them, happily said good-bye to their dear ones, but instead of being sent to the internment camp they were arrested and sent to Auschwitz, where they were killed. An hour later the German police summoned the leading members of the Judenrat—Moniek

Merin; his brother Chaim; his assistant, Fanny Czarna; Dr. Aaron Levenstein; and M. Borenstein. We heard later that they had all been sent to Auschwitz and killed there. The Germans didn't need them any more. The disappearance of the leadership of the Judenrat was a signal that we were approaching our end. A few days later, the Gestapo man Dreier came to the ghetto and nominated Vovek Smetana and others to lead the Judenrat, but we knew that this was only a masquerade.

For us, the "Final Solution" began on August 1, 1943. At midnight, our ghetto was surrounded by German troops. Jews were taken from their houses and bunkers and brutally beaten. On August 2, my family and I were among thousands of Jews taken into the streets, escorted by Gestapo men with machine guns and dogs, and forced to walk to the railroad station in the next town, Będzin. As we were waiting to be put on a train bound for Auschwitz, another transport of some 5,000 Jewish men, women, and children arrived. They were running because they were being beaten by the Germans and were forced to go on the train that had been meant for us. That meant we had to wait 16 hours, the rest of the day and the entire next night, for another train. We really went through hell, not knowing what was happening. Then we were herded into freight and cattle cars, hundreds in each car, packed so tightly that we could not move. I was together with my parents, my sister, my husband, and our five-and-a-half-year-old son. My brother was not with us because he was with the underground group when the Germans came for us. We did not let him know that we were being deported because he would have come to join us. We were hoping that somehow he would survive. But, alas, I found out later that he was caught with three of his friends—Josef Korzuch, Samek Meitlis, and Samek's wife, Lola. They were all shot.

Daily transports were sent to Auschwitz from our town and its surroundings—10,000 people between August 1 and August 6, 1943. The Germans ordered the remaining 1,000 Jews to clean the remnant of the ghetto. The last ones were deported in January 1944. All together 23,000 Jews were deported from my hometown.

A former neighbor of ours, Sarah Lieberman, a nurse, was among the last to arrive. She told me that the Germans, while inspecting the stores in Sosnowiec, found a picture of my brother with some friends, all members of Ha-No'ar ha-Tsioni, in a photographer's place. They looked for these young people, found them in the ghetto, and shot them. Only one was not caught; Dr. Burstyn survived and settled in Israel. He had a copy of this picture and gave it to Kibbutz Tel Itzhak.

As soon as the Germans shoved us into the railroad car, the door was sealed. The train ride from Będzin to Auschwitz normally took no more than two or two-and-a-half hours. We traveled for almost a full day. There was no food or water, just what we had brought with us. There was no bucket for going to the toilet. Literally everything was done in the car. There was one little window in the car because it was a cattle car, and we were treated like cattle. We were nothing but cattle to the Germans anyway—even less because we couldn't be used as meat.

During the hours spent on the train our family tried to sit together like birds on a wire so as not to lose each other. Some people were crying; others were praying to God. Some were cursing God. But our family didn't utter a word. The car was filthy. Hundreds of people were crowded together. No one thought of eating or drinking.

It was a long, tragic journey. In our car was a young nurse from the Jewish hospital of our town, a member of one of the Zionist youth organizations. When she realized that the train was taking us to Auschwitz, she swallowed cyanide and died instantly. She probably knew more about Auschwitz than the rest of us. Maybe she had heard about it from someone who had escaped and had been taken to the hospital. When we arrived at Auschwitz, the Germans took out her dead body, but not her.

CHAPTER 4

Auschwitz-Birkenau

On August 4, 1943, we arrived in Birkenau, the main subcamp of Auschwitz, which was equipped and intended for killing. The train stopped as we reached our final destination, although we did not realize how final it was. The doors of the railroad cars were opened, and we faced SS men holding machine guns and clubs, shouting and beating us. The camp smelled like a latrine. I saw women dressed in striped, gray-blue dresses who moved like shadows. I saw a chimney constantly spitting fire. We were guarded by SS men and women. My husband was holding our little boy. We stood together, behind my parents and my sister. One SS man (I learned later that it was Dr. Rohde) started the selection. With a single movement of his finger, he was sending some people to the right and some to the left. Suddenly, there was terrible chaos and screaming. Men were separated from women. People with children were sent to one side, and young people were separated from older-looking ones. No one was allowed to go from one group to another. My parents were holding onto each other. Our five-and-a-half-year-old son, my little sunshine, went with his father. Something that will haunt me to the end of my days occurred during those first moments. As we were separated, our son turned to me and asked, "Mommy, are we going to live or die?" I didn't answer this question. I didn't know how. First, we didn't know what would happen, and second, how do you answer a child in Birkenau?

After a while, I was left with only my sister, Rozka, among a group of maybe 500 women. The rest of the transport of 5,000 people was gassed right away. Suddenly we 500 women found ourselves alone without the others, without the men, without our parents or children, without anybody. We really didn't know what had happened; we did not expect what was to happen. I, in my naive hope, believed that the rest of my family was experiencing the same thing I was and that I would soon see them again.

My sister and I, like all the other women in Birkenau who were chosen to live, were forced at gunpoint to walk, five in a row, to a bathhouse (called the "Sauna"). There we were ordered to undress, we were washed, and our heads were shaved. Then we were taken to a place called the *Schreibstube,* or administrative office, where numbers were tattooed on our arms. I was given the number 52406 along with a triangle. I have been asked many times whether or not it hurt, and my answer is that it was the least of the pain. I was already numb and did not feel anything. The wound they gave us in our hearts was much deeper and more painful than the tattoo. That was the first stage of our humiliation. At that moment, I lost my name, my identity, and became nothing more than a number. I was nobody. Then we were given some ridiculous clothes and kerchiefs. I had a beautiful long red dress and a short pink apron, like a clown. With my shaved head, I looked so terrible, so alien, that when I stood next to my sister, we didn't recognize each other at first. We were given shoes—clogs, really. They were hard to walk in and so noisy that you could hear someone coming long before you could see the person. When the Polish fall came, and the earth got soft from the rain, when you put your feet into the soil, you couldn't take them out.

After this, we were taken to the women's unit, which was divided into camps A, B, and C. I was taken to Block 14 in Camp A, and my sister to Block 15, but we saw each other every day. Camp A, which was intended for newly arrived women, also housed the hospital, the infirmary, and the dental clinic, as well as the infamous Block 25, where Jewish women who were selected to die in the gas chambers were kept for 24 hours. Also in Camp A was Block 27, known as the *Schonungsblock,* the so-called convalescents' barrack. *Schonung* means protection or "taking care of," and Jewish women released from the infirmary spent a few days in Block 27. The inmates did not want to be there because they were afraid of selections. In fact, however, most were taken to the main camp of Auschwitz to be subjects for medical experiments. Other women from Block 27 were chosen to be prostitutes and taken to a bordello within the camp. Few came back. We never knew what had become of them.

Camp B was for the working units, or "commandos." The main working commandos were Union, the ammunition factory; Canada, where clothing and articles were taken from the arriving prisoners; and Raysko, outside the camp, where the prisoners worked in gardens in order to provide the camp with potatoes and vegetables. The labor units that went outside the camp were made to march to their work to happy tunes played by a small orchestra made up of women inmates. What a macabre irony!

Camp C, also called the Gypsy family camp, was where entire Gypsy families— men, women, and children—were kept. I heard that there were as many as 20,000 Gypsies in Auschwitz. On August 2, 1943, about 3,000 of them were gassed.

Block 14, where I "lived," and the other barracks like it were built like stables. In the center of each barrack stood a long stone stove. On each side were two-story-high bunks where we slept, ten women on a bed, packed like sardines. Our daily food began with a bowl of some kind of herbal tea, although it was called coffee, which was distributed right after the first roll call at 6 a.m. For lunch, we were given a so-called soup that was really mostly water with turnip leaves. It had the odor of a latrine. When I smelled it coming from the kitchen, my stomach turned and I was ready to vomit. In the evenings, after the second roll call, they gave us a piece of black bread, perhaps an eighth or a fourth of a loaf. Once a week we got a very small piece of margarine and once a week a small piece of spreadable cheese that smelled like Limburger. Once in a while we got a little jam or marmalade, but most often we just had the dry bread. As for what was in it, who knows! I was hungry, so I ate it.

In my barrack I met a few of my former patients who had arrived a few days earlier. One of them noticed my bewildered look when from afar I saw a chimney spitting fire. Trying to be merciful, she said, "Dr. Bimko, this is a bakery. There they bake bread." In my terrible ignorance, I believed what she said. How could I bear to think that those flames had reduced my family to ashes? Then, after a few days, I realized that this was the chimney that had spit out the fire that had consumed my parents, my son, my husband, and hundreds of thousands of other Jews. Although we had heard stories about Auschwitz and the other camps, I just could not believe that such a place existed on earth. Then I found a naive answer. Maybe what I had heard as a child was true: that there was a paradise and there was a hell, and that there was probably a war between God and the devil, and the devil won. Therefore, we ended up in hell. Otherwise, how could God allow all this to happen?

It's hard to live with such knowledge, hard to want to live, hard to work, hard to exist. I felt that I was losing my senses. For the first few days after I arrived, I was unable to speak, or eat, or sleep. I was only thirsty. I exchanged three portions of my bread and three helpings of soup with some Polish girls who gave me in return a piece of soap and a toothbrush. But soon hunger overwhelmed me, like everybody else. If I fell asleep even for a few minutes, I dreamed that I was lying under a tree and good, cold water was flowing down.

I tried to keep clean, but it was not easy. I always felt humiliated and ashamed. I hated sleeping in my clothes. I was ashamed to admit that I was hungry. I was ashamed to go to the bathroom and to be exposed half naked in front of so many other women. I was ashamed of the way I looked. I seldom spoke.

There were moments when I thought that I was losing my mind, but one episode restored my sanity. We had to stand outside the barracks at 4 a.m., lined up in rows to wait for the morning roll call, called an *Appell,* which started at 6 a.m. That is when the SS guards counted us. One morning, right after the roll call, a torrential rain came down. We wanted to return to the barracks but instead were forced by the SS women to sit there for hours. As the rain fell down over our bodies, I realized that we were utterly helpless. Tears came to my eyes, the first ones since my arrival. When they mixed with the rain and I sat there sobbing, I found myself again.

The month of August was very hot and we were still in quarantine, not assigned to any work. Every morning we were sent out to sit in a field, called the *Wiese.* As we sat on the grass doing nothing, we tried to shield our bald heads with the kerchiefs, but the SS women who were watching us took them away with sadistic pleasure. Our bald heads and ears, exposed to the burning sun, were soon covered with painful blisters. I watched my little sister suffer in silence, and I suffered, too, because I could not do anything to help her.

When we were ordered to do some work, each group had a different task. I was chosen to carry empty beds from one place to another and back again. There was no reason for it; it was just to keep us occupied. As a result, I became quite an expert at carrying beds. This lasted for about four weeks.

In September 1943 a transport with Jews from Greece arrived. The women were mostly young girls from Salonika. In addition to Greek, they spoke Hebrew and

French but did not understand German. When I went to see them, I met two sisters. The younger one was mute and deaf; when she tried to speak only a scream came from her throat. I cautioned the older girl not to let her sister try to speak because she would not survive once her infirmity was discovered. I can imagine how hard it was. One day while visiting them, I had a terrible experience. I was not afraid to die, but I was always afraid of being beaten. While I was speaking with the girls, an SS woman came in and asked one of them a question. I responded, explaining to her that they did not understand German. She struck me with her club. It happened to hit me in the back of the head, in a spot called the "yellow point," where the visual nerves meet. I fell on the stone floor and lost my sight. I was totally blind! Some of my former patients tried to help me go to sleep, but I couldn't. I was think-ing of how I could get some cyanide so I wouldn't have to go to the gas chamber. As I lay in bed wondering what would happen to me, little by little my vision started to return. First it was a dark gray, then a lighter gray, and by morning my sight had returned completely. After that I saw the Greek girls quite often. To my great satis-faction, they survived. After the liquidation of Birkenau, they were sent to Bergen-Belsen, in Germany, where I met them after liberation.

In the same month a transport of Jewish women arrived from Majdanek. Some came to our barrack. One of them was Lonia, a pharmacist from Warsaw. We soon became good friends, and she told me her story. Her husband was in another camp. They had a little boy my son's age, whom they had left with Polish friends who had promised to take care of him. She always believed that she would find them after the war. Although I thought she was naive to believe in such miracles, I supported her hopes.

At the beginning of September 1943, I became sick with malaria. I suffered from a high fever, probably about 104 or 105 degrees Fahrenheit. Nobody really knows because there was no way to measure it. I also had the red spots that are typical of typhus. I don't know if I got it from the transport of Greek girls or from the terrain, which was wet and full of mosquitoes. Marika, our Czechoslovak *Blockälteste* (the German-appointed barrack matron), who usually wasn't that nice, sent me to the camp hospital, where Dr. Ada Mamlok, a friend from Sosnowiec, helped me recover. I don't think she had any medication, but she washed me and arranged for me to have a bed for myself and a clean blanket. There was nothing else she could do. After about two weeks, I was sent back to Block 14. If I had been at home, I probably would have been in the hospital much longer, but in the camps it was dangerous to be sick for long. While I was in the infirmary, I probably contracted hepatitis, which was not treated. As a result, I still suffer from liver infection. Dr. Mamlok later died of typhus in Birkenau.

After my return to the barracks from the hospital, I learned that a new SS doctor was coming to the Birkenau camp and hospital to make daily inspections and selections. Born in 1911, Dr. Josef Mengele was the son of a rich, old Bavarian Catholic family. A medical doctor, he was interested in anthropology and genetics. A fervent Nazi, he had come to Auschwitz in May 1943. In addition to conducting selections, he worked in the SS laboratories doing research and experiments in genetics. His main interest was the study of and experimentation with twins.

I saw Mengele in Birkenau for the first time in October 1943. He was young, handsome, and very clean, but his sadism and cold cruelty were endless. If he found a person with so much as a pimple during his daily inspections and selections, that person was sent to the gas chamber. With sadistic pleasure, while whistling Wagnerian and other operatic arias, he sent tens of thousands of Jews to their deaths. He was a great lover of music and a sadistic lover of human suffering. He also made selections in the Gypsy camp, sending them to the gas chambers as well. Many of the selections of Jews took place on the eve of Jewish holidays. I remember one on the eve of Yom Kippur 1943, the most sacred day of the year. The Germans were expert at mocking our religion.

A few days after I first encountered him, Mengele called all medical personnel to report for work in the Jewish infirmary—also called the Jewish *Ambulanz*— in Camp A. I was lucky to be among those chosen to go there. Although I had been trained as a dentist, Mengele said that as there were already two dentists, I would have to work as a doctor. (Actually, I had had some medical training because the first year and a half of dental school was devoted to the study of anatomy, physiology, and pathology.) My friend Lonia was also assigned to work as a doctor. The Jewish infirmary was a small barrack where the two of us, two women doctors, and four nurses lived and worked. We welcomed the change; it meant that we could work, that we would each have our own bed, and that we would not have to stand for roll calls. Our task was to attend to Jewish women; we were not allowed to treat non-Jews.

While I was working in the infirmary, I had many opportunities to observe Mengele. On two occasions, he hit me in the face with his hand. One day, a young woman was late for roll call outside her barrack. Mengele ordered her to come forward, knocked her to the ground, and put his booted foot on her chest. Humming an aria from *Madama Butterfly*, he kept his foot there until she was dead. He showed the SS men a new way of killing.

The infirmary was small, with one room where we received patients and, behind a partition, six beds where we slept. It was not very well equipped. There were mirrors for looking into mouths and scissors to cut bandages. We had only some paper bandages, which looked like rolls of toilet paper, and a very few pills, mainly aspirin, perhaps 100 for the whole camp. We also had a little bit of ointment; it looked like Vaseline, but we never really knew what it consisted of. These things came from the SS pharmacy, but we always had to go and fetch them, so I had the privilege of walking around the camp by myself. A Dutch Jewish girl and a Jewish man worked in the pharmacy. I never knew their names, and they never knew mine. They were very good and let me steal from time to time. I stole such things as ether for anesthesia and aspirin. We didn't have to steal the paper bandages.

The women came to the infirmary with abscesses, furuncles, and wounds inflicted by the dogs and whips of the SS guards. We tried to help these women as much as possible. One day a group of 14 young Jewish girls came to the infirmary for treatment. Soon the SS woman supervisor, Drexler, came and took the women away, sending them to the gas chambers. Fourteen young, healthy Jewish girls! We were heartbroken. As a result, we warned the barrack nurses to abstain from sending anyone to us, at least for a short time. We stole some bandages and ointment that we gave to the nurses so that they could help the patients for a little while.

The *Kapo* (inmate appointed by the Germans to head a barrack or commando) of our infirmary was Edith Engelberg, a young Jewish girl from Prague. Her parents had once been owners of a kosher restaurant. She heard that I knew French and Hebrew and asked me to teach her those languages. For this I earned a piece of bread weekly—a small piece, but it was a welcome addition for my sister and me.

One day I became sick. Lonia took care of me, keeping me in her bed. When I started to recover, she came down with the same disease, and naturally, I took care of her. She insisted that the same louse made both of us ill, and that we were therefore related through a louse.

We really had no knowledge of how to perform surgery and did it only when someone's life was in danger. For example, if a woman came in with a leg so swollen that it was bursting with pus and she was on the verge of dying, we had to operate. If a German doctor had spotted her, she would have been bound for the gas chamber and crematorium. So I boiled some instruments and a scalpel. Using the same technique I had learned for treating an abscess in the mouth, I cut the leg, burned out the pus, then put sterile gauze with some ointment over it. Although the bandaging looked very good in the infirmary, it usually burst as soon as the woman took a step outside because it was just regular paper. It was an impossible situation. Elsewhere in the camp, however, even less medical care was available.

Women who were pregnant when they were brought into the camp or who became pregnant were aborted. This was to save the life of the mother, because if it became known that she was pregnant, she would be sent to the gas chambers. A man named Dr. Hermann, who came from Warsaw and was working in the men's clinic, performed many of these abortions. I met him when I went to fetch some fresh blankets for my patients. We spoke through the barbed wire, I told him I needed help, and he promised to do what he could. Even though Auschwitz was surrounded by two barbed-wire chains, very often at night the first one was taken away. We took advantage of this, and one or two nurses and I would walk the women over to Dr. Hermann. He and his colleagues performed the operation, and two or three hours later we took the women back and placed them in a bed where they would be safe. It was easier for Dr. Hermann to abort them than it would have been for us because he worked in a proper clinic that was supervised by the Germans and hence better equipped. Other abortions were performed in the barracks by Dr. Gisella Perl.

Female SS guards who headed the work units came every day. All of them were beasts, particularly Irma Grese. She was young, probably in her twenties, blond, and very beautiful. She always carried a stick and beat people with it. There were also two sisters named Volkenrath; one of them, Elizabeth, worked in the *Magazin*, the supplies depot, giving out packages that arrived for the Poles and others who were not Jewish. Another SS woman, whose name I later learned was Juana Bormann, always walked with a big dog that jumped on the inmates and bit them. I testified against these women at the Belsen Trial in the fall of 1945. All three were sentenced to death and executed.

In 1944 selections took place almost daily. While Dr. Mengele made selections in the hospital, Dr. Fritz Klein made selections in the camp itself. Thousands of Jews were sent to the gas chambers. In April there was a big selection, and all the Jewish patients from the hospital were sent to the gas chambers. The number of infirmary personnel needed was therefore reduced, and Lonia and I were sent back to the camp. We ended up in Block 26, a block for Jewish and non-Jewish women with scabies. Our function was to smear the patients with a liquid called Mitigal. Two beautiful young German girls came to us as patients. Jehovah's Witnesses, they believed in passive resistance because, according to their religion, God was responsible for everything. Even so, they went to the gas chambers just like the Jews. Still, they had to be taken by force and carried onto the truck because this was their way of resisting the SS.

The supervisor of this barrack was a Polish woman from Kraków, Helena Zacha-czewska. She was Jewish but had Polish papers, and the Germans never found out the truth. She was a wonderful person and helped us a lot. Once, she gave us some bread and onions, luxuries that she had received from her family. (Poles were allowed to keep in touch with their families by letters and were allowed to receive food packages.) I shared this food immediately with my sister, and I must admit that was the first night since my arrival in Birkenau that I did not go to sleep hungry.

One day Helena came in with two Polish women. She told us that the women had taken part in the Polish resistance against the Germans in Warsaw. They had been caught, arrested, and sent to Birkenau. In order to spare them from being sent to the *Strafkommando,* the punishment commando, Helena asked us to put their names on the list of patients with scabies, which we did.

In April 1944, right after Passover, a great tragedy befell me. My sister Rozka became a victim of a selection. She hadn't felt well and was in the camp "hospital." This time Dr. Mengele had come into the hospital to make the selection, while Dr. Klein was outside, in the camp. If I had known what was happening, I probably would have had the courage to ask Dr. Klein to save my sister, but I was working in the scabies block, not in the infirmary. After she had been selected, she was held for 24 hours. I went to see her several times and said, "Rozka, I'm doing everything possible to save you." I went to the *Lagerälteste,* Dr. Ena Weiss, and begged her to save my sister, saying, "Ena, she is young; my family, my husband, my child are all gone. She still has a husband somewhere. Save her. Take my number because mine is 406 and hers is 405." She said, "I will do whatever I can," but she never did anything!

I could not save my sister. Helena, who had some connections in the *Schreibstube*, went and begged for me, but it was too late. I did not want to believe the terrible truth. The nights were impossible. Everyone in my block understood my pain, but I was left alone with one more wound that would never heal.

I vividly recall one day in May 1944 when Helena came running to tell us that a big selection was to take place in the camp hospital and that Mengele was on his way. The healthy women would be sent to work in Birkenau and the sick ones to the gas chambers. We were also ordered to form a group of patients who were recuperating. They, too, would be sent to work. We wondered how we might be able to save our patients. Then we had an idea. Helena helped us get the sick inmates dressed in heavy clothes and we sent them out to work on a labor commando. When Mengele came, we said that we didn't have any sick women, that they had all been sent to work. To our great relief, he believed us, and we were able to save all our patients.

At the beginning of June 1944, Mengele called the female medical personnel together, asking each of us if we had had children's diseases. Most of the women answered no. I decided to tell the truth and answer yes. As a result, a few days later I was sent to a new compound in Birkenau called Mexico. The prisoners were mostly young Jewish women from Hungary and a few from Łódź. I was assigned to a barrack with 100 young Jewish girls, 13 to 20 years old, all of whom were sick with children's diseases: measles, scarlet fever, and diphtheria. It was a new experience. With the help of a few nurses and a little medication, we did our utmost to heal them. They were wonderful young people, but our work there lasted only until October.

Mexico was a very small compound, with only a few barracks. The *Lagerälteste* was Adolph Schilling, a German Christian inmate. He was a Communist, arrested by the Nazis in 1933. He had spent the first years in prisons, then Dachau, and finally Auschwitz and Birkenau. He belonged to the elite of inmates, as he was among the first ones to arrive in Auschwitz. He was a good man and helped us a great deal. One day, Mengele arrived at our hospital fuming with rage. He assembled the doctors and nurses and told Schilling that on the way to visit us he had seen six Jewish women who were supposed to be carrying the barrels of soup for us, sitting on the ground and resting. An unforgivable sin! He handed Schilling the stick that he always carried and ordered him to wait for the women and punish them by giving each one 25 lashes. Schilling refused to take the stick. He said: "I don't beat." Mengele was speechless. He did not utter a word. He just looked at Schilling in disbelief.

I was later told that following the liberation of Birkenau by Soviet troops, they found some 650 inmates, most of them sick and unable to walk. There were only a few healthy ones, among them Schilling, who hadn't left Birkenau. After all, the dream of his life was being fulfilled: the Russians had come. When a Soviet officer asked him who he was, before he could answer, somebody cried out: "He is a German." The officer took out his gun and shot Schilling.

Here at Mexico, I was again able to help. Once, we had a group of Hungarian teenaged girls in the infirmary, many of whom were terribly ill. I pushed them to get dressed and go out to work. When Mengele arrived, I was able to present him with a list certifying that all the girls were well and would be sent to a work camp the following day. He left that day without conducting a selection. And later on, when we learned that Mexico was about to be liquidated, once again I got the nurses to help me get everyone in the infirmary dressed, putting the sick inmates among the healthier ones. That way, we succeeded in saving many Jewish women.

In August 1944, I actually went into one of the gas chambers. I had been ordered to fetch some blankets from there, and I took the opportunity to go inside. I had always wanted to see the gas chambers with my own eyes. I testified about this incident at the Belsen trial some 13 months later, as follows:

> It was a brick building and there were trees around in a way as if it were camouflaged. In the first room I met a man who came from the same town as I do. There was also an S.S. man with a rank of Unterscharführer, and he belonged to the Red Cross. I was told that in this first big room the people left their clothes, and from this room were led into a second, and I gained the impression that hundreds and hundreds might go into this room, it was so large. It resembled the shower-baths or ablution rooms we had in the camp. There were many sprays all over the ceiling in rows which were parallel. All these people who went into this room were issued with a towel and a cake of soap so that they should have the impression that they were going to have a bath, but for anybody who looked at the floor it was quite clear that it was not so, because there

were no drains. In this room there was a small door which opened to a room which was pitch dark and looked like a corridor. I saw a few lines of rails with a small wagon which they called a truck, and I was told that prisoners who were already gassed were put on these wagons and sent directly to the crematorium. I believe the crematorium was in the same building, but I myself did not see the stove. There was yet another room a few steps higher than this previous one with a very low ceiling, and I noticed two pipes which I was told contained the gas.[2]

When I was working in Mexico, I heard about Mala Zimetbaum. Born in Poland in 1922, she was still a child when the whole family moved to Belgium. She had arrived in Auschwitz in September 1942 with a transport of Belgian Jews. After the selection she was sent to the women's camp in Birkenau. Mala was a beautiful girl; her hair was not shaved off. She worked as a messenger between the camps, delivering orders of the SS to the blocks. She fell in love with a Polish non-Jewish prisoner named Edek Galinski, one of the first inmates in Auschwitz. He was in touch with the underground and was planning to escape with Mala. One evening in June 1944, Mala came to the Jewish infirmary, washed her hair, spoke to everyone, and left to go to her place. The following day there was a big uproar. All the inmates in both the women's and the men's camps were ordered to stand for roll call. News came that Mala and Edek had escaped. We were counted and recounted, and we hoped that their escape would be successful. But, alas, a few weeks later they were caught at the Slovak border and sent back to Birkenau, where they were sentenced to be hanged. The SS prepared a big spectacle, again ordering all the inmates from both the women's and the men's camps to assemble to watch the executions. When Mala was led to the gallows, she took a razor that she had hidden in her hair and cut the veins on her wrists, to deprive the SS of the satisfaction of killing her. Edek also committed suicide.

The Sonderkommando, a unit made up of Jewish male prisoners, was assigned to the death installations in Birkenau: the crematoria and the gas chambers. Every few months, they were relieved of their duties by being put to death themselves.

---

2. *Trial of Josef Kramer and Forty-Four Others* (The Belsen Trial), edited by Raymond Phillips (London, Edinburgh, and Glasgow: William Hodge and Company, Limited, 1949), p. 68.

In October 1944 a Jewish underground movement that had been set up in Auschwitz in 1943 contacted a Jewish girl, Rosa Robota, who worked in Union, the ammunition factory outside the camp. She, Bala Gertner, and three other Jewish girls smuggled explosives out of the factory and delivered them to the members of the underground and then to the Jews of the Sonderkommando, who destroyed the crematoria. The Jews were arrested and interrogated but never betrayed anyone. Nor did the Jewish girls. They were hanged on January 6, 1945.

I recall many incidents that took place in Birkenau. The following is one of the most inexplicable. A young woman from Lublin named Sophia Litwinska, who was married to a Catholic Pole, had been arrested in 1940, kept in a prison in Lublin for a whole year, and then sent to Auschwitz with her husband in the autumn of 1941. One day she broke her leg and was taken to the hospital. There was a big selection in the hospital block, and Sophia, with many other Jewish patients, was among those condemned to die. Sophia was already in the gas chamber when she suddenly heard her name called. She raised her arm, and somebody pushed her out of that room and covered her naked body with a blanket. It was the German Commandant, Franz Hoessler, who took her by motorcycle to the hospital in Birkenau, where she stayed for six weeks, recovering from headaches and heart trouble caused by the gas. She was told that she had been taken out of the gas chamber because she had come to Auschwitz from a prison with a file card with her personal data. Therefore, it was determined that she could be shot or hanged, but not gassed!

Sophia remained in Birkenau, working in the Canada commando. At the beginning of 1945 she came to Belsen, where we met. She was also a witness for the prosecution at the Belsen Trial in September 1945.

I spent more than a year and three months in Birkenau. It was a time of humiliation, torture, starvation, disease, fear, hopelessness, and despair; a time when Nazi brutality and sadism reached their height. I am happy for anyone who was not in a concentration camp. No matter how much you have read, how many films you have seen, how many stories you have heard, you can never comprehend what just one day in Auschwitz was like, for the truth was always worse than anything one could imagine. I often wonder why there were so few suicides. It would have been so easy just to touch the electrified barbed wire. But what is suicide? Is it an act of courage or weakness?

CHAPTER 5

Bergen-Belsen

O n November 14, 1944, Dr. Mengele chose nine Jewish women to send to another camp as a medical team. I was one of them, as were Hermina Schwarz from Slovakia and Luba Tryszynka and Hela Selzer from Poland. Hermina and Luba had been *Stubenälteste* in different barracks in Birkenau, cleaning the place and giving out food to the inmates. Lonia and I cried when we parted. We exchanged addresses where we hoped to meet after the war.

The nine of us received new clothing and navy blue coats with a red stripe on the back. We learned that our destination was a concentration camp in Germany called Bergen-Belsen, a place we had never heard of. We were convinced that we were going to be killed, and when each of us received a whole loaf of bread, we thought this would be our last meal. As we were waiting to leave Birkenau, a *Lagerälteste*, a woman from Tarnów named Stania Starotska, came up to us and told us that she, too, would soon be going to Bergen-Belsen. She apparently did not like Luba because she said to her, "Wait, when I come to Bergen-Belsen, life will not be easy for you." Luba became frightened, but I told her that I would protect her, which I did. Less than a year later, Starotska was one of the defendants at the Belsen Trial.

Guarded by one SS man with a machine gun and another with a pistol on each side of his belt, we were taken from Birkenau to Auschwitz, where we boarded the train. Our next stop was Katowice in Upper Silesia, a city close to my hometown of Sosnowiec. How tragic it was that even if I could have escaped, there was no place and no person for me to go to.

We had a compartment to ourselves. The following morning we arrived in Berlin. There we were taken to another part of the city in order to change trains. Berlin had been heavily bombed, and we were glad to see the German capital in ruins. When we arrived at the other station, our guards demanded a separate compartment for us. The old conductor said that there were none. When the SS men started to argue, the conductor asked them, "Men, don't you know that there is a war and no time for special treatment? People have to sit wherever they can find space." And so we were pushed into a wagon with many passengers. All of a sudden a young man sitting next to me whispered, "I have a postcard if you want to write to somebody. I promise you I will mail it." I don't know if this offer was a humane gesture or a provocation, but unfortunately, I had nobody to write to. The train then stopped in Hanover.

Konzentrationslager Bergen-Belsen was situated in Lower Saxony, 55 kilometers from Hanover. It was originally established in spring 1943 as a camp for special prisoners (an *Aufenthaltslager,* or transit camp) by order of SS Reichsführer Heinrich Himmler himself. At that time a few thousand so-called privileged Jews arrived in Bergen-Belsen. They were Dutch, Greek, Hungarian, Polish, and Turkish Jewish families, many of whom held visas to emigrate to South or Central American countries such as Argentina, Honduras, Paraguay, and Uruguay. Those families were to be exchanged some day for Germans. They were housed in barracks behind barbed wires on one side of the road that bisected the camp. On the other side of this road were barracks with Soviet prisoners of war. Bergen-Belsen was also intended to be a convalescent camp where sick inmates from other camps were to be sent to recuperate.

In August 1944, 1,000 women arrived from Auschwitz; they were Jewish women from Łódź and Polish women who had taken part in the Warsaw uprising. In September and October more women arrived. They all lived in tents. Finally, they were put in some barracks, which then became the concentration camp for women.

On November 23, the nine of us arrived in Bergen, a village two kilometers from the camp, to which we marched. As we were standing at the gate to enter the camp, I felt that here was not only the end of our road but the end of the whole world. We were registered and received new numbers. Mine was 10060, a number written on a piece of cloth and attached to the left side of my dress—my new identity. Then we were taken to the barrack, which was a type of infirmary, and placed in our new quarters.

I met two Polish women doctors with whom I had worked in Birkenau. They told me that there were 8,000 women in the camp: 7,100 Jews and 900 Poles. Conditions in the camp were terrible: it was filthy; people were hungry and sick, and we were freezing. Whatever was bad in Auschwitz was worse in Bergen-Belsen, except that there were no gas chambers. Ironically and sadistically, the sanitary conditions in this so-called convalescent camp were the worst I ever experienced, as were the food rations, which consisted of a dark liquid called coffee, three-fourths of a liter of turnip soup, and one-sixth of a loaf of bread. The sick became sicker and weaker.

When we arrived the camp commandant was Sturmbannführer Adolf Haas. He was replaced in December 1944 by Josef Kramer, the former Commandant of Birkenau, whom we knew and feared. Kramer set out to make our existence even more desperate. He started with a method the SS had used at Birkenau: roll calls twice a day. The winter was very cold, and standing for hours in the cold, snowy weather drove the inmates to exhaustion and increased the existing diseases.

The SS doctor, Dr. Schnabel, was an old man. He ordered us to start preparations for a Jewish hospital. I was appointed to organize and supervise the hospital, and we started to work. Another Jewish nurse whom I remember well from those desperate days was Hela Losz-Jafe, who had also come from Birkenau. Ours was an impossible task. There was no medication for the sick and very few beds. The sanitary conditions were beyond description. Epidemics raged, and hundreds of people were dying daily. We were desperate. But amid this total desperation, an event resembling a miracle came into my life.

In the midst of a bitter cold December night, we were suddenly alarmed by the noise of crying children and shouting SS men. We were ordered to come out of the barrack, and there we saw a huge truck full of crying children. The SS men unloaded the truck and ordered us to take the children in. There were 49 boys and girls between eight months and 15 years old. We learned from the older children that they were Jews from Holland who came to us from the camp for "internees" situated on the other side of the main road. Their fathers had been sent somewhere in Germany, allegedly to teach the Germans the art of cutting diamonds, and their mothers had also been transported elsewhere. Some of the children had been told, however, that their parents had been killed.

It should not be difficult to imagine our feelings at that moment. We had been given the opportunity to take care of these abandoned Jewish children, and we gave them all our love and whatever strength was left within us. The children were scared and hungry. They asked for bread, but, sadly, we had nothing to give them. We tried to console the children, and finally they fell asleep. But I lay fully awake, thinking about what would happen to the children the following day when the SS doctor came to inspect the hospital.

When Dr. Schnabel came the next morning on his daily rounds, he saw the children and started to shout, *"Was macht das Pack hier?"* (What is this rabble doing here?) I decided to be 90 percent truthful. I told him that the children had been brought to us in the middle of the night by SS men who had ordered us to keep them. My heart was jumping; what would the doctor do? But the Germans always function on orders. He accepted my answer, and the children remained with us except for one eight-month-old boy, who died of diphtheria after a few days. We were heartbroken.

A few weeks later, more Jewish children arrived—21 boys from Buchenwald and some others from Theresienstadt. We also found children in the camp whose mothers had died of typhus. We took them to our place and ended up with 150 Jewish orphans.

As the result of the liquidation of Auschwitz and other labor camps in the eastern part of Europe, thousands of inmates were arriving in Belsen daily. Among them were a few women whom the SS considered too old to work. In order to save them, we took them to the hospital and assigned them as night-watchwomen. That way they were allowed to sleep during the day and were not seen by the SS. They all survived. Among them was Mrs. Losz, the mother of Hela Losz-Jafe, who worked at the children's block and cooked for them.

Our camp became too small, and we were moved to the camp of the former Russian prisoners of war, on the opposite side of the road. The barracks were spacious. Three of them were equipped with beds. In two of the barracks we established a hospital and an infirmary; the third, Block 211, was set aside for the children. They had their own beds, and we lived with them and attended to them day and night. The team that arrived with me from Birkenau helped me keep the children alive. We talked to them, played with them, tried to make them laugh, listened to them, comforted them when they cried and had nightmares. When they were sick with typhus, we sat beside them telling stories and fairy tales. I sang songs to them in

Polish, Yiddish, and Hebrew—whatever I remembered—just to calm them until they fell asleep.

The biggest problem we had was feeding the children, especially the little ones. For many days after they arrived, we had very little food. The children were hungry. One night, two-year-old Johnny Kleerekoper woke up crying, "Mama Ada, give me bread." I was heartbroken because I had nothing to give him.

We sent word of the children to the Jewish men who worked in the SS food depot, and they risked their lives daily to steal food and pass it to us under the barbed wire. We received the same help from the Jews working in the SS pharmacies. They gave us all the medication we needed, and not one of the children succumbed to the raging typhus and other epidemics, although they all went through them. Without these Jewish men and women, the children would not have survived. I feel great admiration and gratitude toward them. In spite of being exposed to subhuman conditions in the ghettos and camps, they had the strength and courage to help others and thereby reclaim their humanity.

Then we encountered another problem. The winter of 1945 was very cruel, and the children desperately needed warm clothes, but where were we to get them? Somebody mentioned that there was a storage room in the camp where clothes taken away from the arriving inmates were kept. I went there with two of the nurses. To my surprise I was greeted and hugged by the two Polish women whom I had helped and protected from heavy work in the scabies block in Birkenau. They gave us all the clothes we wanted.

More than 50 years later, I was reminded of an episode when I confronted the camp Commandant, Josef Kramer. One of the children was a tall, slim boy, age 14. Each time Kramer saw him, he wanted to send the boy to the men's concentration camp. That would have meant the end of him. I had to do something. I said, "Herr Hauptsturmführer, you are a big man, tall. When you were 12 years old, were you already tall or still a little boy?" He just looked at me and walked out. The boy remained with us. His sister wrote to me from a reunion of the children of Belsen in Amsterdam in 1995: "I never forgot your courage when you asked Commandant Kramer to free one of your children."

In December 1944 some of our medical team—two doctors and six nurses—received new, white uniforms from the Germans. They ordered us to come to the entrance gate. After a while two big, black Mercedes limousines arrived. From the first one, four high-ranking SS officers stepped out, and from the other one, two more alit, along with a man in black civilian clothes. They all looked in our direction, then went toward the camp of internees. We could not understand the meaning of all this. Two weeks later, we were ordered to go to the Hungarian Jewish family camp and give vaccinations to the people there because they were due to go to Switzerland. It was our first trip to the camp of internees. On the way we passed all the other camps. We passed the Polish camp. We passed the Jews who had arrived from the "Hotel Polski" in Warsaw. We passed the Dutch camp, the place our children had come from, and the Greek camp. We saw the people standing there, but we were escorted by SS guards and were not allowed to speak to anybody.

In the Hungarian camp, the people told us that the man we had seen in civilian clothes was Rudolph Kasztner, a journalist and lawyer who had become an activist in the Labor Zionist movement, first in Cluj, and then in Budapest. In early 1943 he was vice-chairman of the Zionist Relief and Rescue Committee of Budapest under Ottó Komoly. The committee maintained contact with the Slovakian working group and with some Palestinian emissaries in Istanbul; they were all aware of the Holocaust in Poland and other countries occupied by the Germans, because many refugees from those countries had arrived in Hungary after 1942. The committee, under the leadership of Joel Brand, smuggled some refugees from Poland and Slovakia into Hungary. In March 1944, however, after the Germans had occupied Hungary, Kasztner believed that the only way to rescue the Jews was through negotiations with the Germans. He and Joel Brand made contact with the SS group in charge and, on direct orders from Himmler, succeeded in rescuing 318 Hungarian Jews and later some more from Belsen. I admit that I was skeptical, but when I was in Palestine in 1946, I met two women from this transport who told me that they had all arrived safely in Switzerland, where they were helped by Saly Mayer, the representative of the AJDC in that country, with whom Joel Brand was in touch. After the war, many Hungarian Jews accused Kasztner of having put his family and friends on the train first. He lived in Israel until 1954, when he was murdered by a Jewish nationalist extremist.

Our working day in Belsen started at 6 a.m.—seeing the children, making rounds, visiting all the hospital barracks. One day at the beginning of January 1945, I came into the infirmary and saw a young Jewish woman lying on the operating table, crying. The woman had a severely infected abscess on her foot and had been sent for surgery by the SS doctor. She told me that she was afraid to be operated on without an anesthetic. I calmed her down, then ran to the pharmacy under the pretext of fetching paper bandages and stole a bottle of ether. The woman was operated on and recuperated. At that time, I did not know her name or anything else about her.

At a reunion of survivors in the mid-1990s, two women came over to me. The older one said, "I am Sarah Berkovitz and this is my daughter. You probably don't remember my surgery in Belsen in January of 1945." The daughter started to thank me for helping her mother. I was embarrassed. I looked at her and said, "I am happy to see you. I saved her for you!" Sarah Berkovitz told me that she had written a book entitled *Where Are My Brothers?* in which she described this episode in a chapter called "A Friend in Need."

Whenever a new transport arrived, the two nurses and I had to go with stretchers to take out the sick people and bring them to the hospital. One day I found a dear friend of my sister's, Hela Weinstein (now Margines), among the new arrivals. She used to spend more time in our home than in her own and loved my family. I told her to pretend to be sick so that I could take her with me. She gave me photos of my family and my first child, which she had kept together with pictures of her own family. She was able to keep these pictures because she was in a labor camp, not a concentration camp, where everything was taken away. I am grateful to her and treasure these photographs. When she heard that my sister Rozka had been killed in Birkenau, she cried bitterly. When she became sick with typhus, in a state of high fever, she constantly repeated, "I want to have tea from Mrs. Bimko" (she meant my mother). So I boiled some water, telling her, "This is tea from my mother." Hela was comforted and drank the "tea." After the war, Hela settled in Israel, where she married and had a son. The family eventually moved to Los Angeles. Hela and I still keep in touch.

There was another incident that sounds almost unbelievable. A Jewish woman who arrived on a transport from a labor camp approached me and said she had heard that we had Jewish children in our compound. She wanted to see if her son was among them. I looked at her, thoroughly amazed that anyone could still believe in miracles. I asked her name and that of her son. She was Dora Lubliner from Łódź, and her son's name was Jacob, called Kovi, now nine years old. I got a peculiar feeling; we had a boy his age and with that name among the children, but I was afraid to give her false hope. Maybe it was her child, but maybe not. So I said, "Yes, we have children. I will take you to them and you can see for yourself." I brought her over to our camp and the miracle happened! She found her son. The scene of their reunion is hard to describe.

She was placed in one of the barracks and was smart enough to leave Kovi with our other children, whose living conditions were better than hers—they were not starving and were cared for with love. After the liberation, Kovi's father, Dr. Michael Lubliner (later the principal of the high school in the Bergen-Belsen Displaced Persons camp), who had survived in another camp, came to Belsen, and the family was happily reunited. Eventually they all immigrated to Los Angeles.

I had another experience in Belsen that still remains an enigma for me. One day, the new SS doctor, Horstmann, told me to go to a small barrack to give an intravenous calcium injection to some unnamed man. I went with a heavy heart; who knows what kind of injection it was? When I arrived, I met an elderly French couple, a Monsieur and Mme Kranach. I told them why I had come, and Mme Kranach gave me the filled syringe. I asked her who had given it to her, and she said she had brought the serum from France. Once I knew that the serum was legitimate, I gave Monsieur Kranach the injection. From then on, I went there every second day. They had a room for themselves with an electric stove, and she always made me a cup of tea. I never found out why they were kept there or why they received such special treatment. After the liberation, they returned to France.

With the Soviet army close by, the Germans liquidated Auschwitz on January 18, 1945, and sent many of its inmates on foot to Bergen-Belsen. Those who made it were exhausted from the long journey, starving, and sick with innumerable diseases. Many were suffering from frostbite. With the transports came the monstrous SS guards and doctors whom many of us already knew only too well. They turned Belsen into an indescribable hell. The conditions in Belsen were at their worst six weeks before liberation. The camp was overcrowded. Typhus, tuberculosis, and other epidemics raged. In the hospital and throughout the camp about a thousand people a day lay on the floors, starving and dying. A small group of inmates and I, who had survived typhus and other diseases in Auschwitz, had developed a natural immunity to these epidemics. The small crematorium could not cope with all the corpses, even though it was kept burning day and night. The unburned corpses were strewn all over the camp. The SS, who felt that their end was near, cut off the water and electricity. We were given one piece of bread per person only three times a week and one-half bowl of so-called soup daily. On top of this, the Germans kept us in mortal fear by telling us that the camp was surrounded by mines and that we would be blown up if we tried to escape. Such was our situation on the eve of liberation. Disease, starvation, despair, fear, and not a single ray of hope.

On April 12 we saw from a distance that the SS men were burning some papers. That is why there are no documents from Bergen-Belsen. The Germans successfully destroyed them. The following day we saw many of the SS guards leaving the camp. They were later captured by the British, returned to Belsen, and eventually tried in September 1945 at Lüneburg. The few guards who remained wore white armbands on their left sleeves. Rumors spread that the camp was about to be declared neutral as a result of negotiations between the German Military Commander and the Commanders of the Allied Forces. Nobody knew what this meant or where this news came from. In any event, we did not believe it. However, on Saturday, April 14, 1945, we received Red Cross parcels—one package for every six people. We began to hope that something was actually happening.

CHAPTER 6

"Hello, Hello. You Are Free."

Then came April 15, 1945. I will never forget that day. It was Sunday, a very hot day. It was strange; there was nobody to be seen outside the barracks. The camp seemed to have been abandoned, almost like a cemetery. I was sitting with the nurses and children, telling them stories. I was desperate. I never believed that we would be free from German slavery, but the miracle happened. Suddenly, we felt the earth tremble; something was moving. We were convinced that the Germans were about to blow up the camp. The children were frightened and crying, and we had a hard time calming them down. We all believed that these were the last moments of our lives. It was 3 p.m. We heard a loud voice repeating the same words in English and in German: "Hello, hello. You are free. We are British soldiers and have come to liberate you." These words still resound in my ears. We ran out of the barracks and saw a British army vehicle with a loudspeaker on top, driving slowly through the camp. The same words were repeated over and over again. Within minutes, hundreds of women had stopped the car, screaming, laughing, and crying. The British driver, Captain Derrick Sington, cried with us. It seemed to be a dream. How tragic it was that the great majority of the inmates were too sick to understand what was happening.

Soon the hysteria and the euphoria were over. There was joy, yes—we were free, the gates were open—but where were we to go? The liberation had come too late, not only for the dead, but for us, the living, as well. We had lost our families, our friends, our homes. We had no place to go, and nobody was waiting for us anywhere.

We were alive, yes. We were liberated from death, from the fear of death, but the fear of life started.

The British tanks rolled on in pursuit of the German army, leaving a group of Hungarian SS guards in charge of the camp for one day. On this one day, they killed 72 Jews and 11 non-Jews. Many were killed trying to pick up a few potato peels lying around the kitchen. Because of this, our family began a new tradition, introduced by my late husband Yossel and followed by our son, Menachem, and his wife, Jeanie. At Passover, we always put potato peels on our seder plate in addition to the bitter herbs *(maror)* to remember those who were killed and to remember what a blessing it was at Auschwitz and Bergen-Belsen to have a potato peel.

The British came back on April 17, this time to stay. They found 58,000 inmates—men, women, and children—90 percent of them Jews. Most were living skeletons, too ill and too weak to walk, sick with typhus, tuberculosis, and hunger. In addition, there were 10,000 unburned corpses lying around the camp. Brigadier General H. L. Glyn Hughes, Chief Medical Officer of the British army, came to see the camp, and I was asked to take him around. (I did not know any English at that time, but luckily he spoke French.) What he saw was a sea of crying bones. At the sight of the dead and near-dead, the general, a medical officer hardened to human suffering, cried unashamedly. He decided on the spot to try to save as many as possible despite the conflicting needs of the military casualties for whom he was responsible. After he read a report in the press that the concentration camp inmates were getting 800 calories daily, he published the following letter in the London *Times:*

> Sir,
>
> At the present time there are frequent references, both in the Press and in BBC reports, to conditions that existed at Belsen and other concentration camps; there are heard such remarks as, "Even the miserable skeletons at Belsen received 800 calories."
>
> May I point out that such statements are entirely misleading and incorrect? Rather should it be said that the maximum ration originally allotted per person in these camps amounts to 800 calories, but the unfortunate internees were very lucky if they ever received this amount. "The miserable skeletons" at Belsen had received neither food nor water for many days prior to the liberation of the camp and very much less

than 800 calories for a long time before this, in spite of the fact that ample supplies were available on the spot and adequate personnel existed for administration and distribution. It is only right that these acts should be made clear at a time when frequent references are being made to the scale of rations in Germany and elsewhere.

Whenever he described his initial impressions of Belsen, General Glyn Hughes said, "The first hours and day will always remain a nightmare for me."

Not far from the concentration camp were German military barracks, strong brick buildings with all the necessary amenities. General Glyn Hughes decided to transform these buildings into a hospital for 17,000 patients and living quarters for our Jewish orphans and the other inmates of Belsen who had miraculously survived. I was asked by General Glyn Hughes and Colonel James Johnston—who was also a medical doctor—to organize and head a medical team from among the survivors. Eight doctors and 620 still-convalescent men and women answered my appeal for help. Only a few were certified nurses, and most of them were still weak, but they all worked with great devotion together with the British army doctors, nurses, and other personnel under Colonel Johnston's remarkable leadership.

Two months later, on July 23, 1945, Colonel Johnston, who remained a dear friend until his death in the mid-1980s, wrote these comments that reflect the conditions under which we were working after the liberation:

> Dr. Bimko was one of the very few people among the 50,000 interned in Belsen who, in spite of all the horrors she had undergone, was still capable and was doing a magnificent job amongst the thousands of sick and dying. I cannot speak too highly of her work in this camp against difficulties which no doctor can ever have experienced before—a complete lack of instruments and medicaments, even of the absolute essentials—beds, blankets, clothing. She had organized her own staff of nurses and was quite outstanding amongst all the other doctors in this camp.
>
> I therefore appointed her to be Senior Interne [sic] doctor in Belsen, in the new hospital areas which we established then,—this task she is still carrying out today. Her duties were manifold and included the drafting

up of suitable doctors and nurses from the horror camp to the new hospital areas, the organization and control of this work in those areas and, in general, to administer the very large non-British medical staff. This task she has carried out at all times most magnificently.

After the sick were disinfected, 17,000 patients were transferred to the new hospital. We also transferred our children, who were placed in two buildings, RB6 and RB7, with bright, spotlessly clean rooms, white sheets on the beds, good food, and constant medical attention. The British were wonderful to them. A Major Smith, who was not Jewish, visited the children quite often. One day he arrived with a truck packed with toys. He told us that he had driven to the nearby town of Bergen and had gone from one German house to another asking if there were children. If there were, he asked that each child take out a toy to give to the Jewish orphans in Belsen as atonement for the wrong their parents had done to these Jewish children. He collected an enormous number of toys and brought them to our children. We, for our part, did everything to teach the children to laugh and play again.

I did not live with the children because I had to be in the hospital near the patients and the doctors. At first I had a small room in Block 55, and then moved to *Kantine* (Canteen) 2, but I visited the children very often. One day they invited me to lunch. When we sat down at the table, two girls put before me a white china bowl with mashed potatoes. I looked and started to cry. In the days before liberation, they once asked what I would like to eat right after the war. I told them that I would like to have a clean white china plate full of mashed potatoes. At that moment I was almost unable to eat.

Our patients were transferred to 66 buildings in the new hospital area, and some into a well-equipped former German hospital. It is not difficult to imagine how the patients felt having been taken out of the filthy barracks and put into clean beds, in airy and well-lit rooms, with medical attention day and night. The British medical team, helped by our doctors and nurses, performed the superhuman task of saving thousands; however, within two months after liberation, 13,944 died; they are all buried in the mass grave of Belsen.

On May 8, 1945, the war in Europe ended. I have often been asked how we felt on that day. I do not remember much—we were so busy with the sick and the dying. Of course, we were glad to hear the news of the Allied victory, but we in Belsen did not celebrate on that day. For years, I have seen a film on television showing the world's reaction to the end of the war. In Times Square in New York, in the streets of London and Paris, people were dancing, singing, crying, embracing each other. They were filled with joy that their dear ones would soon come home. Whenever I see that film, I cry. We in Belsen did not dance on that day. We had nothing to be hopeful for. Nobody was waiting for us anywhere. We were alone and abandoned. Fifty years later I expressed these feelings at the United States Holocaust Memorial Museum in Washington, D.C., on the anniversary of V-E Day.

In the meantime, mass burials took place daily. Big pits were dug, large enough to hold 5,000 and more corpses. The dead bodies were loaded onto trucks and brought to the burial sites. The mostly interlocked and disintegrating corpses—which were infected—were placed into these mass graves. When the task proved to be too enormous to be done manually, the dead were shoved into the pits by bulldozers driven by British soldiers. The SS men who had been arrested at Belsen were now forced by their British captors to arrange the bodies in rows. Before the mass graves were closed, Dr. Isaac Levy, Senior Jewish Chaplain of the British Liberating Army; Rabbi Leslie Hardman, another British chaplain from Leeds; and Rabbi Hermann (Zvi) Helfgott, who had been a Yugoslav POW, recited kaddish. The pits were closed and signs were put up noting the numbers of bodies in each: 5,000, 2,500, 2,000, 1,000, and so on. The burials must have brought emotional relief to many survivors. The British meant well: they were punishing the tormentors and forcing them to look at their victims. But I was very sad. Why, even at the last moment, couldn't our dead have a decent burial? Why did they have to be touched by the murderers? I felt that this was a sacrilege, but, unfortunately, there was nobody else to do it.

At the end of the war Rabbi Helfgott was one of several Jewish officers in Marshal Tito's underground army. In April 1945, he and three others came to Belsen shortly after the liberation. One of them, a Mr. Nandorf, was searching for his wife. I looked up her name on the list of our patients, and it turned out that she was in the same block where I lived, Block 55. The encounter of the two was more than dramatic. He was shocked when he saw her, because she looked like a skeleton covered with skin. She weighed only 38 kilos. She was one of the patients fed intravenously, and she had survived only thanks to the care and devotion of our medical team.

Rabbi Helfgott remained with us and helped the other two military chaplains perform the burial rites for the dead. He joined the DP camp's Jewish Committee and became head of the Belsen Rabbinate. In 1948 he left with a group of young men to take part in Israel's War of Independence.

Colonel Spottiswoode of the military government was so moved by all he had seen that he decided that the neighboring German population should also witness the horrors of Belsen. On April 24, 1945, Germans from the nearby towns and villages were brought to see the open burial pits filled with bodies and skeletons. The SS men and women, with the SS doctor Fritz Klein in front, were paraded on one side of the yawning grave, and the German mayors stood on the other side. The loudspeaker was brought and they heard the following words:

> What you will see here is the final and utter condemnation of the Nazi Party. It justifies every measure which the United Nations will take to exterminate that Party. What you will see here is such a disgrace to the German people that their name must be erased from the list of civilised nations.
>
> You who represent the fathers and brothers of German youth see before your eyes a few of the sons and daughters who bear a small part of the direct responsibility for this crime. Only a small part, yet too heavy a burden for the human soul to bear. But who bears the real responsibility? You who have allowed your Führer to carry out his terrible whims. You who have proved incapable of doing anything to check perverted triumphs. You who had heard about the camps, or had at least a slight conception of what happened in them. You who did not rise up spontaneously to cleanse the name of Germany, not fearing the personal consequences. You stand here judged through what you will see in this camp. You must expect to atone with toil and sweat for what your children have committed and for what you have failed to prevent. Whatever you may suffer, it will not be one-hundredth part of what these poor people endured in this and other camps. It is your lot to begin the hard task of restoring the name of the German people to the list of civilised nations. But this cannot be done until you have reared a new generation amongst whom it is impossible to find people prepared to commit such crimes;

until you have reared a new generation possessing the instinctive good-
will to prevent a repetition of such horrible cruelties.[3]

The Germans saw the mass graves, but *naturally* they had never known anything!

On May 8, the mass burials were over, and a new cemetery for single graves was
established in the area of the new compound in what was known as Camp 2. The
first person buried in a single grave was Dr. Henryk Lieberman from Sosnowiec,
on May 10, 1945.

By May 21, we had completed the transfer of the patients from the notorious
Camp 1 to the barracks in Camp 2. All the other inmates who were able to take
care of themselves had also been relocated to the barracks near the hospital. On
that day the British burned down all the barracks of the concentration camp in an
effort to stop the spread of epidemics. A special ceremony was held. Somebody
put a huge photograph of Hitler on Barrack 44. Then Dr. Johnston ceremonially
fired the first shot into Hitler's photograph, and the old camp was set on fire. Two
notice boards had been erected by the British on either side of the entrance gate,
one in English and one in German, with these words: "This is the site of the infamous Belsen concentration camp liberated by the British on April 15, 1945. Ten
thousand unburied dead were found here; 13,000 have since died, all of them victims of the German New Order in Europe and an example of Nazi culture." Years
later the boards were stolen, but photographs of them remain.

The burning of the old camp marked the beginning of regular medical attention
for the sick and our new life. In addition to the British military personnel and our
own medical staff, we were assisted by a unit of the British Red Cross, the Swiss
Red Cross, and a group of Quakers. Ninety-seven medical students from Britain
also came to help us. They were led by Dr. A. P. Meikeljohn, an Irishman who
brought both enthusiasm and human sympathy to his task.

After the British medical students left, 150 Belgian medical students came to
Belsen. The epidemics in Belsen allowed the students to observe symptoms of diseases rarely seen elsewhere. The students were wonderful. Their relationship with
the sick was touching, and they were liked by everybody. Army doctors also came
to the hospital and asked to be allowed to have a look at the spots that were symptoms

---

3. Derrick Sington, *Belsen Uncovered* (London: Duckworth, 1946), pp. 89–90.

of typhus. It was a happy day when we could announce the end of the exhibition; the epidemic was over.

I also recall a young British psychiatrist who came to offer his help. I told him that I did not know if we had patients for him, that I was ignorant about his field of medicine. Our main task was to save the sick, to heal the body first. Noticing his eagerness to help, I suggested that a nurse show him around but told him he would have to find patients by himself. After a few hours, he reported happily that he had found a patient. I knew the girl well and was surprised to hear that she needed his help. Then he said, "I saw a beautiful young girl looking into a piece of broken mirror and combing her hair with a broken comb." When I asked him why he found this so peculiar, he repeated his observation. I said that he should give the girl a whole comb and a whole mirror; if she refused, then he had a patient. He realized his mistake and was genuinely ashamed.

We urgently needed more doctors and nurses. We were hoping that some Jewish doctors in the United States would close their private practices for a little while and come to help us, if only for a month. To our great disappointment, none came. I still can't understand why. The British were obliged to accept German medical personnel. The German doctors arrived still in their military uniforms, but they were not SS. Most patients, especially women, were shocked to see them, and at first refused to be examined or treated by them, but they had no choice but to accept them. The German doctors rendered good service, and some of them remained to the end, when the camp was closed. The work of our own doctors and nurses remains a great example of self-sacrifice. It is astonishing how they found enough strength and energy to care for the sick while they themselves had not yet fully recovered. Of great assistance to our work of physical rehabilitation was the help we received from the Swedish government and the Swedish Red Cross under Count Folke Bernadotte. They accepted 6,000 of our patients for recuperation in Sweden. But not all the sick survivors reached Sweden; 72 died on the way to the ships and are buried in the ancient Jewish cemetery in Lübeck.

The work of the British army doctors and nurses, the voluntary organizations and medical students, and our own medical team was a ray of light in those dark days. Those who recovered remained forever grateful for the humanitarian service that was performed with such tremendous generosity.

Shortly thereafter, the epidemic subsided; patients partly recovered. Hospital beds gradually emptied, and we were left with the main hospital and its 400 beds to serve the normal requirements of the camp. The 66 former hospital buildings became living quarters, and slowly people started to leave. The Czech, Dutch, French, Greek, and Yugoslavian Jews were repatriated, but the Hungarian, Polish, and Romanian Jews remained in Belsen, refusing to return to their countries of origin. We were now considered displaced persons (DPs). A few children were lucky enough to find a relative alive; the rest remained with us. Engrossed in the administration of the hospital, hoping for the day the epidemics would end, I could not imagine life outside the camp.

A few days after the liberation, I heard that among the survivors of Belsen was a group of men from the area of my hometown. I went to see them, hoping to find a member of my family. In Block 88 I found my brother-in-law, Manek Rosman. We cried together, especially when I told him about the tragic death of his wife, my sister, Rozka. Many weeks later, he came to see me, saying that he was going to our hometown to take care of his family's former house. I described where we had buried a few valuable things, and when he returned to Belsen he brought me the gold jewelry that he had been able to find. I kept only a few items that had been handmade by my beloved father, including my mother's wedding band and my own. I sold the other items and shared the money equally with Manek. For my share I was able to have a new pair of shoes and a winter coat made for me by a shoemaker and a tailor in Belsen.

I started to chain-smoke right after the liberation. I was busy from before six o'clock in the morning until after midnight, going from one barrack to another to see the patients, to talk with the doctors stationed there, to find out what was needed, how they felt. I supervised the doctors and volunteers from among the survivors who cared for 17,000 sick men and women. I used to come back to my room after a whole day of not having eaten, absolutely ravenous. A girl from my hometown whom I had saved was waiting with a cup of tea. The tea she got from the British, and I had a bottle of whiskey that one of the British doctors had given me. The British also gave us cigarettes. That was the first time I learned how to smoke in spite of having been a student for so many years. So I smoked a cigarette, drank a little whiskey and a cup of tea, and slept for a few hours. The following morning it started all over again. Nobody ever saw me without a cigarette. I only gave them up years later, after Yossel had stopped smoking.

CHAPTER 7

Yossel

S ome time in late April or early May 1945, I heard that three days after the
liberation, 200 Jewish men had assembled in Block 88 and had elected a Jew
from Będzin named Josef Rosensaft, whom everyone called Yossel, as their
spokesman before the British and that they had formed a temporary Jewish Committee of what was now the DP camp, based in Block 4 on the other side of Belsen.
I then started to receive invitations to meetings of the committee, signed by this
Yossel, which were brought to me by his secretary, a man named Itzhak Eisenberg,
but I ignored them all. I simply could not imagine that there were any healthy Jews
anywhere in Belsen. One day, Rabbi Isaac Levy, one of the British chaplains, asked
me to come to a meeting of the Jewish Committee that evening, which was being
combined with a farewell party for another chaplain, Rabbi Leslie Hardman. I decided to go. There I met Yossel for the first time.

When I arrived at the meeting Yossel was singing a Yiddish song, "In the Desert,"
about a man who walks on the hot sand of the Sahara Desert and suddenly sees
fields, forests, and trees. He admires the beauty but soon realizes that it is only a
mirage. The same happens in life; you sometimes meet a person who seems to be
nice, smiling at you, and you trust him, but you soon find out it is all an illusion. His
next song was a revolutionary one, calling people to take arms and to fight for life.

Rabbi Hardman asked Yossel about the religious feelings in the camp. Did people
believe, or did they express disillusionment? Yossel answered him with a story. One
day he was sitting in Birkenau with a group of other Jewish men, among them the

Rabbi of Zawiercie, a very pious man. It was evening, after roll call and a selection. Outside, trucks were rolling, taking hundreds of Jewish men and women, crying and screaming, to the gas chambers. The rabbi heard their voices. With tears in his eyes, he suddenly said, "You know, God can also be sometimes a liar." Everybody was shocked. The rabbi continued: "If God were to look down on us now and see what is happening, He would say, 'I did not do this,' and that would be the lie."

I observed Yossel. Here was a man of small stature, but when he spoke, you saw a giant. His blue eyes were almost transparent. You thought you could look through him, but after a while, you had to stop. Something told you not to go any further. I was impressed by this man's demeanor, his actions, his fast decisions, and by his Jewish pride and dignity. He had a strong will and a wonderful sense of humor. He loved children and cared for the needs of others. I soon came to love him and to know that he loved me.

The son of Deborah and Menachem Mendel Rosensaft, Yossel was born on January 15, 1911, in Będzin, Poland, very close to my hometown of Sosnowiec. Yossel's parents belonged to a prestigious Hasidic family. Like my own parents, they were disciples of the Rabbi of Ger. His mother was the daughter of the wealthy Yankele Szpiro of Będzin. Deborah was well educated and very energetic; she worked in the family scrap metal business. Reb Mendel was extremely pious, and a scholar. Unfortunately none of his writings were saved.

Mendel Rosensaft was also legendary throughout our region of Zaglembia and beyond for his charitable deeds. He was always ready to help the needy—the orphans, the sick, and the homeless. Although he was strictly observant, he never hesitated to break the Sabbath in order to help a Jew or a Jewish family that was facing a crisis.

Yossel was the youngest of six children, with three sisters and two brothers. At the end of World War I, when Yossel was only seven years old, his mother died during a typhoid epidemic. His father never remarried, and Yossel was brought up by his oldest sister, Leah, whose husband had died in the same epidemic. He received his early education at a *heder* in Będzin and was then sent to study at a prestigious yeshiva in Warsaw under Rabbi Meir of Plotzk and Rabbi Menachem Zemba. After he finished his studies, Yossel returned home to work in the family business. He joined the left-wing labor Zionist Po'alei Zion movement. Shortly before the war, he married Bronka Bajtner, a widow with an eight-year-old daughter.

When World War II broke out, Yossel was in Warsaw with friends. After the German occupation of Warsaw on September 27, 1939, Yossel came back to Będzin and remained there until 1943. Realizing that a tragic end for the Polish Jewry was approaching, he was able to obtain three visas to Paraguay through friends in Switzerland, but he did not use them because he did not want to leave his father and the rest of the family behind. During Passover of 1943, they were still together, but shortly thereafter all the Jews of Będzin were sent to the Kamionka ghetto in a suburb of Będzin, and almost all Yossel's relatives were deported, never to return. Only his father remained.

On June 22, 1943, Yossel, his wife, and her daughter were part of a transport of a thousand Jews sent from Będzin to Auschwitz. Unusually, this was not a freight or cattle train but a passenger train. A window was half open, and his wife begged him to jump out so that he could try to help them. Yossel was an excellent swimmer (he had been the only Jewish member of a Będzin sports club). As the train was rolling over a bridge across the Vistula River, he was able to escape through the window and landed in the water. As he was diving, the SS men riding on the roof of the train spotted him and started to shoot. Three bullets hit Yossel: one grazed the front of his forehead, the second lodged in the wrist of his left hand, and the third penetrated the upper side of his leg. Somehow, he was able to swim away into the darkness. After a while, he came out on the other side of the river, bleeding. He did not know where he was or where to go. It was already dark. He started to walk, spotted a dim light, and heard the barking of a dog. When he approached the light, he saw a little peasant's hut. Should he go in? Would they let him in? Maybe they would denounce him to the Germans. But he had no choice and decided to try his luck. An old Polish woman opened the door to his knock, saw him, and screamed. She crossed herself, but let the bleeding man in. She gave him coffee and some water to clean his wounds. He used his underwear as bandages. She let him dry his clothes and gave him her son's cap. With this cap on his head, his blond hair, and his blue eyes, he looked like a Pole. As soon as the morning light appeared, he thanked the woman and started to walk; he finally arrived back at the Będzin ghetto, where he found his father bent over the *Gemara*. He had been fasting since the last of his children was taken away, praying and hoping for his son's return. When he saw Yossel, he did not utter a word. He just kissed him and went to the morning prayer service.

Yossel soon realized that his escape had been in vain. Nothing could help those who had been deported. A doctor removed the bullet from his wrist, but the one in his leg was located too close to a vein to be removed safely. The Będzin ghetto was liquidated on August 1, 1943. On that day, Yossel's father died in his arms. Yossel buried him in the backyard and smuggled himself into the nearby town of Zawiercie, but not for long. On August 27, 1943, he was deported from there to Birkenau. His number was 149594. The prisoner who tattooed his arm made a mistake. Instead of putting the number "5," he wrote another number, then crossed it out and wrote the "5" over it, and that was how his tattooed arm looked.

After Yossel arrived in Birkenau, with the help of the underground movement he and two brothers from his hometown, Zev and Abraham Londner, posing as electricians, went to the women's camp to try to find out if his wife or any of their relatives were there. They were caught and interrogated for eight days in the notorious Block 11, known as the Bunker of Auschwitz, the so-called "Death Block." They were then sent back to Birkenau. A few months later, Yossel learned that a group of Jewish men was going to be sent to work at Lagisza, a labor camp only a few miles away from his hometown, and he was able to get himself included in that group.

In March 1944, he made up his mind to escape again. He persuaded some of the Polish civilians who came daily to work in the camp to help him. Two of them brought him civilian clothes, which he put on over his striped prison garb, and the Poles smuggled him out inside a large water pipe. He returned to Będzin, where he found shelter at the home of a Polish friend named Marzec. He remained free for six weeks, until the end of April 1944. Planning to flee to Hungary, he was on his way to meet a man who was going to provide him with the necessary forged documents, but he was caught and returned to Auschwitz. As an escapee, he should have been executed, but the Germans were anxious to find out who had helped him escape and where he had been hidden in Będzin. He was interrogated daily for seven months in Block 11. Much of that time he was imprisoned in a tiny "standing cell" with six other inmates. The Germans applied the worst tortures—beatings, hanging by his arms, electric shocks—but Yossel did not betray those who had helped him. It was a miracle that he survived. The Anglo-Jewish journalist Joseph Fraenkel later wrote about Yossel, "Here is a man who, like Dante, was in the 'Inferno' and returned."

The story of Block 11 is described in the "Log" of Auschwitz, which was smuggled out of Auschwitz in 1944 by two Polish members of the resistance group, Jozef Cyrankiewicz, later the Prime Minister of Poland, and Stanislaw Klodzinski. According to this account, the Germans had installed a punishment commando in the cellar of Block 11 as early as 1940. Among the Jewish prisoners in the Bunker were some who had tried to escape and others who had lived on the Aryan side with Aryan papers and were caught. In the backyard of Block 11 was a wall against which prisoners were shot. At the time of Yossel's arrest, the *Kapo* of the Bunker was a Jew, Jacob Kozielczyk, a boxer who had once apparently trained Max Schmelling. On Yom Kippur 1944, he ordered Yossel to lead the prayers. All the Jews in the Bunker, Jacob among them, attended, and Yossel, half-naked, chanted Kol Nidre. Yossel had a beautiful voice. He also chanted the prayers the following day. His voice should have reached and shocked the heavens. To break the fast, Yossel earned a portion of sweet soup from Jacob, not only for himself, but for all the Jews in the Bunker.

Yossel's work assignment was to clean the hall. One day while mopping the floor he heard somebody calling his name. Although it was forbidden to approach a cell, he did so and found Yadzia Schwimmer, a pretty young girl from his hometown. She cried when she saw him. She told him that she had lived as a Polish woman, on Aryan papers, but was caught by the Germans and sent to the Bunker. She begged Yossel to help her get out. Yossel went to the *Kapo*, told him the story, and persuaded him to send Yadzia to a working commando in Birkenau. She survived, came to Belsen, and joined a group of young people who went to Israel and established the kibbutz, Nezer Sereni.

Yossel told us that one day Dr. Jacob Edelstein, the chairman of the Council of Elders in the Theresienstadt camp, was brought to his cell in the Bunker. He had been dismissed from his post because—so the charge read—there was a discrepancy between the registered Jewish population of Theresienstadt and the actual figure. In December 1943, he was deported to Auschwitz with his family, and they were all shot on June 20, 1944. When the commandant of Auschwitz, Obersturmbannführer Hoess, came to take him to his execution, Edelstein slowly put on his jacket and proceeded to shake hands with each of the other inmates. When Hoess yelled at him to hurry up, Edelstein replied: "Pig! I am the master of my last minutes, not you." Edelstein's words expressed the spirit that guided Yossel in his work and his life. Later, the high school in the Belsen DP camp was named in Dr. Edelstein's memory.

When the Soviet front was moving toward Kraków, not far from Auschwitz, the Germans got nervous. On November 14, 1944, they emptied the Bunker and let all the prisoners into Birkenau. After seven months in the Death Block, Yossel was assigned to a punishment guard unit. He had to wear a special uniform, a jacket with a big red spot in front and another in back, with the initials I.L., for *im Lager* (inside the camp), indicating that because he had tried to escape, he could not be sent on any work detail outside the camp.

As the Germans started to liquidate Auschwitz and Birkenau, Yossel was first taken to Langensalza, a forced labor camp in Thüringen, and from there to Dora-Mittelbau, a subcamp of Buchenwald and a veritable hell. Finally, he arrived in Belsen on a death march in early April 1945. He and his group were not sent into the concentration camp itself because it was overcrowded. Instead, they were kept in a compound in the nearby German military barracks, where they, too, were liberated by the British on April 15.

ABOVE: *(left to right)*
Hadassah's son, Benjamin
(Beni) Prejzerowicz;
her brother, Benjamin
(Yumek); her parents,
Hersh Leib and Hendla
Bimko; and her sister,
Rachel (Rozka). Sosnowiec
ghetto, 1941 or 1942.

RIGHT: Hadassah's son,
Benjamin.

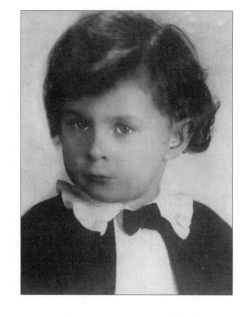

ABOVE: Hadassah's high school class; Hadassah is standing, second from the right, behind the seated teacher. Sosnowiec, 1926.

BELOW: Members of Ha-No'ar ha-Tsioni in Sosnowiec, *(left to right)* Dr. Burstyn, Yumek Bimko, Samek and Lola Meitlis, Josef Korzuch. Sosnowiec, 1942 or 1943.

ABOVE AND BELOW: Hadassah in Nancy, France, 1934.

LEFT: Shortly after the liberation, *(from left)* Hadassah with Colonel James Johnston, fellow survivor Dr. Ruth Gutman, and another British officer. Belsen, May 1945.

ABOVE: Hadassah *(center)*, standing between Earl Harrison *(left)*, President Truman's special representative charged with reporting on conditions in the DP camps, and Josef Rosensaft. Belsen, July 1945.

ABOVE LEFT AND RIGHT: Aboard the SS *Champollion* to Palestine, April 1946.

LEFT: Hadassah *(left)* and Josef *(right)* pose with one of the teenage orphans *(center)* who is about to leave the Bergen-Belsen displaced persons' camp on the first authorized children's transport to Palestine, April 1946. The group sailed aboard the SS *Champollion* from Marseille.

USHMM

RIGHT: Josef and Hadassah on their
way to meet members of the United
Nations Special Committee
on Palestine. Belsen, May 15, 1947.

USHMM, courtesy of Nederlands Instituut voor
Oorlogsdocumentatie

BELOW: Members of the Central
Jewish Committee in the British
zone on their way to the mass graves,
(left to right) Berl Laufer, Hadassah
and Josef, Norbert Wollheim,
Paul Trepman, and Raphael Olewski.
Belsen, 1947.

USHMM, courtesy of Nederlands Instituut voor
Oorlogsdocumentatie

ABOVE: Josef Rosensaft addressing the Second Congress of Liberated Jews in the British zone of Germany. Dr. Noah Barou and Norbert Wollheim are seated at left. Shlomo Adler-Rudel, Hadassah, and David Rosenthal are to the right. Bergen-Belsen, July 1947.

USHMM, courtesy of Nederlands Instituut voor Oorlogsdocumentatie

ABOVE: At right, Hadassah *(center)* in a classroom of the Belsen school, with Vida Kaufman *(right)* of the AJDC, 1947 or 1948.

LEFT: Hadassah and Josef under the *hupah* at their wedding. Lübeck, Germany, August 18, 1946.

BELOW: Hadassah and Josef with their newborn son, Menachem, in the Glyn Hughes Hospital at Belsen on May 6, 1948, five days after Menachem's birth.

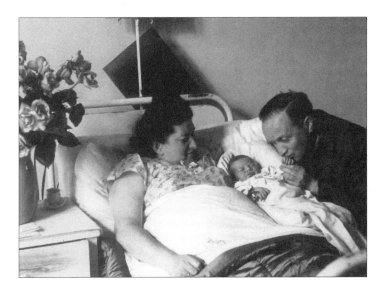

CHAPTER 8

We Organize Ourselves Politically

Under Yossel's leadership, the Jewish DPs of Belsen were determined to be a self-governing community with autonomous social and religious institutions, and freedom to assert Zionist policies and to pursue them by action. Three fields of activities engaged our energy from the very beginning until the final hours of our stay in Belsen: (1) our physical and spiritual rehabilitation, (2) the search for our families, and (3) political activities. We were determined to be recognized not as displaced persons but as Jews, and we were committed to support the Yishuv, the Jewish community in Palestine, in its struggle for independence. We knew it would be a long time before we all would be able to leave Belsen.

Palestine was under the British mandate and almost closed to Jews, while other countries were reluctant to accept Jewish survivors. They were as indifferent to our tragic experience as they had been before and during the war. Realizing that our stay in Belsen would be a long one, we organized ourselves into a temporary community. I was asked to join the Jewish Committee of Belsen, which I did, and in September I also became a member of the Central Committee of Jews in the British zone, which served simultaneously as the Jewish Committee of the Belsen DP Camp. Yossel was chairman of both committees. I was appointed head of the Health Department.

A dedicated core group served on these committees. The principal members of the first Jewish Committee of Belsen, which functioned from shortly after the liberation until the first Congress of Liberated Jews in the British zone in September

1945, included, in addition to Yossel and myself, Berl Laufer, Itzhak Eisenberg, Rabbi Zvi Helfgott, and Paul Trepman. The leadership of the first Central Committee, which was in office until July 1947, included Norbert Wollheim, from Lübeck, as vice-chairman; Berl Laufer as secretary; and Carl Katz, from Bremen, and Samuel Weintraub as joint heads of the Economic Department.

We established a children's home, a kindergarten, an elementary school, a high school, a vocational school with evening courses for advanced students, and a religious school. Our teachers deserve special recognition, as they worked for months without books. Only later were they helped by members of relief organizations and the Jewish Brigade, a group in the British army composed of Jewish volunteers from Palestine. Although the British denied us the permit to do so, by July 1945 we were publishing a Jewish newspaper, *Undzer Shtime (Our Voice),* edited by Paul Trepman, David Rosenthal, and Raphael Olewski. The first issue was handwritten and mimeographed. In 1947, it became a weekly called the *Wochenblatt.* We also published more than 60 books, periodicals, and brochures.

We had a rabbinate representing moderate orthodox and ultra-orthodox religious views, but they worked well together and showed a great deal of tolerance for one another. The secretary of our rabbinate, Cantor Moshe Kraus, later became the first Chief Cantor of the Israel Defense Forces. We also had a library, sports clubs, a Jewish police force, and a legal department. In legal matters, we were helped by Dr. Hendrik Van Dam, the legal adviser to the Jewish Relief Unit in the British zone and later Secretary General of the Central Council of Jews in Germany. We had a drama studio, called the "Kazet Theater," directed by Sami Feder, a Jew from Poland. All the actors were amateurs who had never performed before, but they were very good and were even invited to perform in Belgium and France. We also established a convalescent home in Bad Harzburg with cultural programs directed by Yecheskel (Chaskel) Saender. All these institutions were run by the survivors themselves.

Yossel gave many of our colleagues nicknames, badges of honor expressing their characteristics. For example, Itzhak Eisenberg, secretary of the Belsen Committee, was called "the Matchmaker," because of his efforts to bring Yossel and me together. He told us later that some other men had given him letters they had written to me, but that he had never delivered them. The editors of our newspaper became known as the "Three Musketeers." Samuel Weintraub, an Orthodox Zionist, was known as "the Saint," and Berl Laufer as "the Redhead," for obvious reasons. Berl was stubborn, honest, and outspoken. Once a man came to Yossel and asked him for some money. Yossel gave it to him. After the man left, Berl said to Yossel, "Do you know that this man has more money than you have?" Yossel replied, "You see, my father used to say that it is sometimes better to give charity to one who doesn't need it than, God forbid, to refuse someone who really does need it."

Max Silbernik and Romek Zynger, in charge, respectively, of clothing and food distribution, worked diligently and rendered extremely valuable service to the Jewish DPs of Belsen, although they were not members of the committee. Thus, our team was like a bouquet of wildflowers: different characters, different backgrounds, but coming together to make our temporary stay in Belsen easier.

Our task of caring for the Jewish survivors at Belsen was made more difficult because of the negative, even hostile, attitude of the first British commander of the DP camp, Major James Jones, toward Yossel and the rest of us Jews. Jones had a British colonial attitude toward the Jewish DPs and treated us as if we were idiots. Under the influence of Polish liaison officers, he wanted us to be governed by the non-Jewish Polish Committee although there were only 900 Poles in Belsen but about 10,000 Jews. We, the Polish Jews, did not want to be Polish citizens any more. Major Jones refused to speak to Yossel as chairman of the Jewish Committee, or to other Jews for that matter, through an interpreter. He demanded that all Jews learn English. He provoked an arrogant answer from Yossel, who once told him to his face, "How about you learning Yiddish? It is easier for one person to learn Yiddish than for 10,000 to learn English." Jones just did not like Jews, and his actions were very hostile toward us. For example, at one point he withdrew the car allocated to Yossel as chairman of the Jewish Committee and refused us a license to issue our newspaper.

Major Jones was finally removed. His replacement, Major Desmond Murphy, was a wonderful person, Irish by heritage, born in the United States, and educated in France. He helped us in every possible way. For instance, when our young men went to Palestine illegally, they had to travel by bus to the American zone to join others. They needed gasoline, which was controlled by the British. Major Murphy was told that the young men were going to our agricultural school. Although he knew the truth, he pretended to believe the story and ordered the gasoline stations to provide whatever gas they needed. He even came to see the boys off. When he said good-bye to them he said, "Don't forget to write me a postcard when you reach your destination."

Then Major Murphy left Belsen and other British camp commanders came. One of them was Simon Bloomberg. He was not only the military commander of Belsen but also the director of UNRRA (the United Nations Relief and Rehabilitation Agency), which at that time administered the DP camps. He was a Jew and the former British governor of Jamaica. He came to see Yossel and asked his advice about his work in Belsen. Yossel told him that he had to decide by whom he wanted to be kicked out: if he was good to us, the British would remove him, and if he followed the British policies, we would get rid of him. Bloomberg remained, and we worked well together.

In June 1945, Norbert Wollheim came to Belsen to see Yossel. Born in Berlin in 1913, Norbert had studied law at the University of Berlin. As a young man, he joined the Zionist youth movement. He did some voluntary social work and also learned spot welding, a trade that helped him later in Auschwitz. After *Kristallnacht* (November 9–10, 1938), he was one of the organizers of transports of several thousand Jewish children, between 12 and 18 years of age, to England. He accompanied the last transport to London in February 1939 and then returned to Berlin.

His parents were deported in 1942 and killed. In 1943 Norbert was deported to Auschwitz with his sister, his wife, and their little boy. The others were killed, and he was sent to the Auschwitz subcamp, Buna-Monowitz (also known as Auschwitz III), where artificial rubber was produced. When the Germans liquidated Auschwitz on January 18, 1945, prior to the approach of the Russian army, his group was sent to Mauthausen on one of the death marches, then to Sachsenhausen, and then to northern Germany. On May 2, 1945, they were liberated near Schwerin by the American army. Norbert went to live in Lübeck and started to organize Jewish life there. Norbert represented the German Jewish communities with whom we worked closely (a phenomenon unique to the British zone) and soon became vice-chairman of our Central Jewish Committee and our dear friend. (Yossel affectionately called him "Yecke," a name that eastern European Jews called German Jews.) He was particularly helpful when our patients were taken to Sweden soon after the liberation, and in 1947 at the time of our confrontation with the British over the return of the passengers of the *Exodus* to Germany. In Belsen, he met a young Jewish woman, Friedel, who was also from Berlin, and they married in 1947. Norbert later also brought the first lawsuit on behalf of Jewish Holocaust survivors against the German company, I. G. Farben, which had used Jews as slave laborers at Buna. Eventually he, Friedel, and their two children immigrated to New York, and we remained close friends. In 1977, Friedel died after a long, painful illness.

In spite of all we went through, there were many highlights during our stay in Belsen. The first happy event was the wedding of a young couple from Łódź in June 1945. They had been engaged before the war and found each other again in Belsen, where they were both liberated. Rabbi Vilensky from England expressed his wish to officiate. Everything was prepared for Sunday. On Friday afternoon, the rabbi came to me, saying that the wedding could not take place until the bride went to the *mikvah,* the ritual bath. There was no proper *mikvah* in Belsen or any other place nearby, but the rabbi was obstinate. I became angry and told him that the wedding would take place; as far as I knew, any Jew could perform a marriage ceremony. The news went around. Many Jewish British officers arrived on Sunday to be part of this happy event. The rabbi eventually gave in. It turned out to be an anti-*mikvah* wedding that took place on Freedom Square in Belsen, under a blue sky. It was the beginning of life.

As Rosh Hashanah and Yom Kippur were approaching, we decided to create a place to worship together. The big movie theater in Belsen was turned into a synagogue. Hundreds of people came, prayed, and cried together, remembering our families, so brutally killed. The cantor, Joseph Mandelbaum, chanted El Moleh Rachamim, the prayer for the dead, which must have penetrated heaven. I have never heard it sung so beautifully.

Many delegations from abroad visited Belsen. In July 1945, Earl G. Harrison, the dean of the University of Pennsylvania Law School, came as an emissary of President Truman to explore and report on the situation of the DPs in Germany. He met with Yossel, Norbert Wollheim, and myself, representing our committee. Also present at that meeting was Reverend Isaac Levy, Senior Jewish Chaplain of the British army, who openly criticized the British policies in Palestine toward the Jews. As a result of Earl Harrison's report, President Truman asked the British government to admit 100,000 Jews to Palestine.

Also in July, a papal nuncio came to Belsen, bringing the message that the Vatican was willing to help us with food and clothing. He spoke French, so I was asked to translate. I thanked him for this offer but said, "We shall manage with the little we have. But the Vatican," I said, "could and should help in a different way." During the war some Christian families had taken in and saved Jewish children. After the war most of these families returned the children to the surviving parents, but others refused to do so. We wanted the Vatican to appeal to those families to return the Jewish children to their relatives. I mentioned two specific cases. In Belsen I had met two Jewish women from Poland, both of whom had left their baby daughters with Christian neighbors. Helen had expected to get her five-year-old girl back, but the Polish family, once her friends, refused to surrender the child. Helen went to court in Poland, seeking her rights. While sitting there and listening to the deliberations, she realized that she was losing her child. She left the court before the verdict was announced, abducted her sleeping child from the cottage where she was living outside Kraków, ran until she came to the railroad station, and boarded a train. After a few days, she arrived in Belsen with her pretty little girl. It was a new world, full of strangers, her mother included, but the child went to our school, started to play with other children, and was happy. In 1948, she and her mother joined Helen's brother in Israel.

The story of the other woman is a sad one. Luba, too, had left her daughter with Polish friends in Starachowice. In June 1945 she went back to Poland to look for her child, who was nine years old by then. Luba was not welcomed by her former Polish friends. On the contrary, she found an antisemitic atmosphere. The Polish family refused to give her the child, who had been brought up to hate Jews. When Luba said to her daughter, "I am your mother and I would like you to come back to me," the little girl responded, "You are lying. You are a dirty Jewess. You can't be my mother. I already have one." Luba went to court, lost the case, and lost her child. She returned to Belsen heartbroken. I asked the papal nuncio to meet with Luba, to talk with her and help her, but nothing happened. She went to Israel with her new husband but never had another child. Her daughter presumably still lives in Poland.

Our temporary community numbered about 10,000 Jews, but this number grew. Thousands of Jews who had managed to escape from Poland during the war and had survived in Siberia and other parts of Russia made their way to Belsen. Among them were 200 children whose parents had died in Russia; we took them into our children's home. Many Jews also came from Hungary, Romania, and Poland, including refugees of the tragic Kielce pogrom and others who had gone back to their country of origin after the war, hoping to find friends or relatives and a place to stay but encountering only antisemitism and bitter disappointment. A special movement, called the Brichah, was founded to bring these people over the border to Belsen and other DP camps in Germany and Austria.

It was not easy to absorb thousands of new arrivals, among them invalids and children with no means of support, but we accepted them with open arms. At first the British refused them DP status, which would have enabled them to receive food rations and made them eligible for emigration. We shared our provisions with them and negotiated with the British on their behalf, finally succeeding in having them classified as DPs.

Fiorello LaGuardia, the former mayor of New York, visited Germany in his new capacity as head of UNRRA, to investigate the situation of the DPs and refugees. The British purposely omitted Belsen from his itinerary. General Evelyn Fenshaw, head of UNRRA in the British zone, was responsible for this. But when LaGuardia came to Hanover in August 1946, Yossel went to see him and told him about the condition of the Jewish DPs in Belsen.

While under the jurisdiction of the British occupation authorities in Germany, we had to depend to a large degree on UNRRA and later on the International Relief Organization (IRO). We had many conflicts with them, especially because of our refusal to be labeled as civilian victims of the war or as refugees. We regarded ourselves no longer as Poles, Hungarians, or Romanians but as Jews, survivors of the declared German war against the Jewish people. As survivors of that war, we insisted that we were entitled not merely to material help but also to freedom and the right to determine our own future. For a long time, the British resisted our demand to be recognized as Jews and refused to give Belsen the status of a Jewish DP camp. Belsen had become a powerful symbol; they knew that a plea from Belsen would have an impact on the world's opinion. To weaken this impact, they tried to change the name from Belsen to Hohne, the name of a nearby village, and to liquidate Belsen by transferring thousands of Jewish DPs from Belsen to other DP camps and centers in Germany. About 2,000 Jews were sent to the town of Celle, not far from Belsen, shortly after the liberation. In May 1945, the British decided to send another 1,127 to Lingen, and 2,000 to Diepholz, both international DP camps near the Dutch border. We were all outraged. Yossel and some of the other members of the Jewish Committee went to these camps to see the living conditions there, which were disastrous. Yossel told the Jewish DPs to return to Belsen, and they were happy to do so. Called before a military court for disobeying orders, Yossel defended himself, saying to the judges, "You liberated us from slavery and we became free people again, so we have the rights of free people to decide about our lives and future. I am representing my people, my fellow Jews in Belsen, and I will not accept orders against them." Yossel was acquitted. Eventually, the Belsen Jewish Committee succeeded in winning recognition and sovereignty as a Jewish community. On instructions from London, Belsen became a Jewish DP camp, an extraterritorial unit in Germany over which the Germans had no jurisdiction. The British finally came to understand and respect us because the issues were not of trivial import but related fundamentally to principles of human justice and political liberty.

In June 1945 several Jewish relief organizations came from abroad to help us in our work of rehabilitation. The first was the Jewish Relief Unit from Great Britain, headed by Leonard Cohen from Manchester and Lady Rose Henriques from London. To Lady Rose, an assimilated Jewish woman, this was a team of social workers, and she showed little understanding for our tragic experiences. The Chief Rabbi's Religious Emergency Council in England sent us two rabbis, Rabbi Vilensky and Rabbi Baumgarten. I never understood why, since we had our own rabbis, and the British rabbis really did not understand what needed to be done. At the beginning of July 1945, when food in Belsen was still rationed and in very limited supply, the two rabbis came to see Yossel, carrying a huge package. They greeted him excitedly. "Reb Yossel," one of them said, "you see this package? Today is the happiest day of my life. The Chief Rabbi in London sent us two knives for ritual slaughtering. From now on the Jews in Belsen can eat kosher meat." Yossel looked at them and asked simply, "Did he also send you a cow?"

The first director of the Jewish Relief Unit in Belsen was Jack Brass; he was followed by Sarah Eckstein. The members of the team were mostly young Zionists who helped at the children's house, vocational schools, and hospitals. The Jewish Agency for Palestine was represented by Kurt (Daniel) Levin, who later became the Israeli Ambassador in Burma and the Netherlands. M. Kraicer, from Canada, was director of HIAS, the Hebrew Immigrant Aid Society, which was helping people immigrate to countries in the Western hemisphere. Joseph Mack, director of ORT, the Organization for Rehabilitation through Training, worked in the vocational schools. The AJDC, also known as the "Joint," one of the most important relief organizations, brought us the first supply of food in July 1945. When we learned that the food from the Joint was available only for Jews in DP camps and not for German Jews living in cities and towns, who, we knew, were also suffering a severe shortage, we shared our supplies with them. The European Director of the AJDC, Joseph Schwartz, an outstanding American Jewish leader and a great humanitarian, visited Belsen often and we became friends.

Jacob Trobe, an American Jew from New York, was the AJDC director for Germany in the beginning. He was a very good man, but in December of 1945, when the British General Frederic Morgan, who worked closely with General Eisenhower, made insulting remarks about the Jewish refugees from eastern Europe, Trobe defended Morgan, and the AJDC had to relieve Trobe of his position. The first AJDC director for Belsen and the British zone was Maurice—known to us as Moshe—Eigen, who developed excellent relations with our Jewish Committee. He left in October 1945, when his wife gave birth to their first child.

The AJDC team included many other good people, a few of whom deserve special notice. Joe Wollhaendler, a young man from New York who just had been released from the army, arrived with a very limited knowledge of Judaism. He learned a great deal in a short time and became almost a "super-Jew." On the front of his jeep he inscribed the Hebrew slogan *Am Yisrael Hai,* the Jewish people live. He was willing, helpful, and a lot of fun. Vida Kaufman, an experienced social worker from New York, was surprised to encounter an organized community when she arrived at Belsen. She was particularly interested in children and schools and worked closely with the teachers. Vida earned the honorary title of "American DP." She lives in New York and never misses a get-together of the *Belseners.* There was also Dr. Fritz Spanier, a German Jew who had gone to Holland after Hitler's rise to power and was one of the passengers of the *St. Louis,* on which he had served as a medical doctor. In Belsen he organized a hospital and a group of fine and devoted nurses. He helped many patients and remained in Belsen until the DP camp was closed in 1950.

Other AJDC directors came and went. The last and very best one was Sam Dallob, a Jew from New York. He had a good heart, understood our problems, worked closely with us, and was always willing to help. He became our close friend. He used to go with Yossel to the British authorities and as a result of a funny incident replaced Norbert Wollheim as Yossel's interpreter. One day, Yossel, Norbert, and Sam Dallob, in his capacity as AJDC director, went to Celle to see Major Wood, the British officer responsible for our food supplies. Yossel asked the major to provide more food for the war refugees, but Wood refused. Yossel became angry and said in Yiddish to Sam and Norbert, "Let him go to hell." The major requested a translation. Norbert replied, "He said that you are a very nice man." Yossel understood enough to know that the translation was not accurate. That was the end of Norbert's career as an interpreter, and Sam Dallob took over. On such occasions, Dallob introduced himself by saying, "Today, I come only as Mr. Rosensaft's interpreter and not as the director of the AJDC." Sam remained with us until the very end, when Belsen was closed.

Some of the soldiers of the Jewish Brigade came to see us from Belgium, where they were stationed at the time. We were all excited to see Jews in uniforms with a Star of David on their arms. Josef Arnon and Shmuel Efron were the first to arrive, in June 1945. Arie Wishniak and Yehoshua Begun worked with the Zionist youth group. Menachem Erlich was a Hebrew teacher in our school; he was killed in the War of Independence in Israel in 1948. Ben Yehuda, also a teacher, stayed with the children in their home in Blankenese, and Arieh Simon, principal of the Ben-Shemen school in Israel, stayed for a short time. Eighteen of our youngest Jewish orphans went to his school after they arrived in Palestine with me in April 1946.

Our most important ally and source of support in our political struggle was the World Jewish Congress (WJC). Its presidents were Rabbi Stephen Wise (until his death in 1949), and then Dr. Nahum Goldmann. We were closest to the British Section of the WJC, and particularly to Dr. Noah Barou, chairman of the WJC's European Executive. Other key personalities of the British Section were Alex Easterman, its political director, and Sidney Silverman, its chairman, a courageous Labour Member of Parliament who often spoke up against his government's policies. We also worked closely with Dr. Gerhart Riegner, who headed the WJC office in Geneva. Their first delegation came to Belsen shortly after the liberation. Among them were Barou, Silverman, Easterman, Rabbi Kopul Rosen, a wonderful lady named Ruth Shaerf, and a Russian-English Jew named Jack Poznansky.

Ruth Shaerf became one of our closest friends. She lived in London and had two sons who worked in her business, a factory that produced nylon fabrics. She opened her house in London to us, and we were always welcome there. Our son, Meni, called her "Grandma Ruth." In later years, Ruth spent many summers with

us in San Remo. She died in Cannes in December 1965, shortly after she had celebrated with us the 20th anniversary of our liberation.

Noah Barou, an economist and a socialist, had been a leader of the Po'alei Zion
movement in Russia before and during World War I. He came to London in the
early 1920s as director of the Cooperative Moscow Narodny Bank. When he was
supposed to return to Russia, he decided to stay in London and asked the British
for asylum, which was granted him. He married a Russian Jewish divorcee with
two children whom he adopted. In the World Jewish Congress, Barou helped us
Belseners fight for our freedom and dignity. He was our loving father, brother, and
haver (friend). He was available to us in person and by telephone 24 hours a day, in
good times and bad.

On July 11, 1947, 4,500 Jewish DPs from various camps and Jewish refugees
came to Marseille and boarded the *President Garfield,* a ship bound for Palestine.
The passengers all wanted to enter Palestine as illegal immigrants. When the ship
was at sea, its name was changed to the *Exodus 1947.* Before reaching Palestine,
the ship was intercepted by the British and forced to go to Haifa, where the passengers were forcibly removed. They resisted and went on a hunger strike. Three
Jews were killed and many wounded.

On July 20, the passengers were sent back to Port-de-Bouc, France, where they
remained for a whole month, suffering from overcrowding, unsanitary conditions,
and the heat. Finally, the British foreign minister, Ernest Bevin, decided to send
these survivors of the Nazi Holocaust back to Germany. Our committee in Belsen
held mass demonstrations in the camp and organized a protest march in the port
of Hamburg, where the *Exodus* was docked. We tried to communicate with the
Jews on board the ship, to let them know of our support and our efforts to help them.
Dr. Barou joined hundreds of *Belseners* on this march. The Hamburg Regional Com-
missioner, Vaughan Berry, knew Dr. Barou because they both were members of the
Fabian Society. Berry greeted Barou in a friendly manner. Barou replied by saying,
"Isn't it tragic under what absurd conditions socialists must sometimes meet again?"

As we were all standing at the port, we heard the shocking news that the people
from the *Exodus* were to be sent to camps behind barbed wires. Brigadier A. G.
Kenchington, head of the Prisoners of War and Displaced Persons Division of the
military government for the British zone at that time, was never sympathetic to

our problems. Yossel, Barou, and Wollheim went to see him. Barou, filled with shame, said to him, "Since the day when I became a British citizen, I have always felt proud to be a citizen of a country which has held high the ideals of decency and humanity. I do not hold you personally responsible for the decisions which were made in London and which you have the sorry task of carrying out. But now the time has come to prove that brutality is the distorted, and humanity the true face of England. Free those people, whom you have provoked into fighting and resistance for their cause."[4]

In September 1947, the British troops removed the passengers from the *Exodus* at gunpoint and took them to camps Pappendorf and Am-Stau, not far from Lübeck. In November, they were transferred to two other camps, Emden and Sengwarden, north of Wilhemshaven. We were constantly in touch with them and helped as much as we could.

Dr. Barou was with us on many occasions. When the Belsen Jewish DP camp was closed in September 1950, he was with us, and in 1955, when we marked the tenth anniversary of liberation of Belsen and a tree was planted in the Judean Hills in Israel, he came to be with us *Belseners*. He died soon after his return to London. In 1957, Yossel dedicated our book *Belsen* to Dr. Barou's memory with the following words:

> Noah Barou was one of the first among the free Jews who came to see us after the liberation. He gave us not only his knowledge and his wisdom, but most important his heart. He shared our sorrows and our joys, as one of us; he identified himself with us completely. He never wearied of listening to our troubles and his devotion lasted out until the last Jews left the camp. To me, and to all of us, he remained a close and dear friend when things returned to normal. Now he is no more, and a light has gone out of our lives.

We were invited to become equal members of the World Jewish Congress, which enabled us to have direct contact with the British government. Whenever we had

---

4. Quoted in Norbert Wollheim, "Belsen's Place in the Process of 'Death-and-Rebirth' of the Jewish People," *Belsen* (Tel Aviv: Irgun Sheerit Hapleita Me'Haezor Habriti, 1957), pp. 65–66.

misunderstandings with the British administration in Germany, with General Evelyn Fenshaw, head of UNRRA, or with Brigadier Kenchington, a WJC official would go with us to meet with members of the British government in London who were more sympathetic to our problems, including Hector McNeil, Minister of State at the Foreign Office; Lord Henderson, Under-Secretary of State responsible for the British zone of Germany; John Hynd, Chancellor of the Duchy of Lancaster, who was responsible for the Control Office for Germany and Austria; and Michael Stewart, who years later became the British Foreign Secretary. In addition, Colonel Robert Solomon, a Jewish lawyer from London appointed in April 1946 as Adviser on Jewish Affairs to the Control Office, was both sympathetic and extremely helpful whenever we needed his assistance.

CHAPTER 9

The Belsen Trial

Following the liberation, the British arrested all the SS personnel, members of the command, and staff of Auschwitz and Belsen, including Josef Kramer, Commandant of Birkenau and Belsen; Franz Hoessler, Commandant of Auschwitz; SS doctor Fritz Klein; and the infamous SS guard Irma Grese. Thirty-seven SS guards and eight former prisoners, *Kapos,* and informers were found in Belsen and on the roads nearby. On September 17, 1945—ironically, Yom Kippur, the Day of Judgment—they were put on trial in Lüneburg, not far from Belsen. This was the very first war crimes trial of the Nazis by a British military court. The court consisted of five judges, presided over by Major-General H.M.P. Berney-Ficklin. There were four prosecutors and 12 court-appointed defense counsel, all British military officers, and 31 witnesses for the prosecution, including eight British officers from among the liberators and 23 survivors. I was persuaded by Brigadier General Glyn Hughes to testify.

The trial was carefully prepared. In April 1945, only days after the liberation, a British officer, Major Geoffrey A. J. Smallwood, was appointed by the Judge Advocate General's Department to investigate what he called the "alleged atrocities at Belsen." He eventually testified as a witness for the defense. The defense attorneys argued that the SS had only obeyed orders. Another officer, a Colonel Smith, tried to argue that the accused had not committed war crimes in the technical sense of that term. I was outraged that the killers of hundreds of thousands of Jews in Auschwitz and Belsen were given such consideration. I simply couldn't understand the concept of a "fair trial," the principle that every accused, even the most brutal murderer, was entitled to a defense. It was especially puzzling to me since there could be no question as to the guilt of individuals like Kramer and Klein, who had been taken into custody at Belsen, the very scene of their most recent crimes.

When I was introduced as a Polish woman, I asked for a correction. "I am a Jewish woman from Poland," I said. I testified at length about my experiences at Birkenau and Belsen. I described the selections conducted in my presence at Birkenau by SS doctors Rohde, Tilot, Klein (one of the defendants in this trial), König, and Mengele. I approached the accused and identified by name Kramer, Klein, Hoessler, Irma Grese, Elizabeth Volkenrath, another SS woman—Stanislawa (Stania) Starostka, the *Lagerälteste* from Birkenau, and three others. I also identified five other defendants, whose names I did not know, as having been at Birkenau. I was asked by one defense counsel whether the nonmedical SS personnel present at selections in Birkenau were under the direction of the SS doctors. I testified that I did not think so because I remembered that on occasion, the SS men would point out a particularly weak inmate and tell the doctor, "Here is one you overlooked." I also testified that Hoessler chose women from among the inmates to be sent into brothels for the Germans.

When one defense lawyer accused me of inventing a particular incident, I answered in anger, "Who was in Auschwitz, you or me?" The presiding judge smiled at this reply. (I later learned that this exchange was reported in some detail in the *New York Times* on September 23, 1945.) Another defense counsel asked me if it was true that Dr. Fritz Klein had given us Red Cross parcels. He wanted me to answer yes or no! I asked the president of the court for permission to answer the question by explaining the real situation and was allowed to do so. I told the court that on the day before the liberation, each barrack in the hospital received two Red Cross food parcels. Dr. Klein and the other SS personnel who remained in Belsen knew—we did not—that the British were expected to take over the camp at any hour. In order to provide a positive alibi for himself, he gave out those parcels in the last minutes. But he had not distributed the parcels before then although they had arrived at the camp many months earlier. When the British troops opened the storehouses after liberation, they found hundreds of those parcels, stacked up to the ceiling. They had been sent from Geneva by the Swedish and International Red Cross but never reached the inmates.

I had the satisfaction that in his closing speech to the court, Colonel Backhouse, the principal prosecutor, referred specifically to my testimony. "I particularly rely on the witness Dr. Bimko," he said. "She, in my submission, is a particularly reliable witness, a professional woman who did magnificent work in Belsen, and, we are told, is still there at the hospital, and her evidence I would ask you to accept."[5]

The trial ended on November 17, 1945. Eleven of the defendants, including Kramer, Hoessler, Klein, Grese, Bormann, and Volkenrath, were sentenced to death by hanging and were executed the following month. Nineteen others, including Stania Starostka, were sentenced to various terms of imprisonment, from life to one year, and 19 were acquitted.

Because the Belsen Trial was the first war crimes trial of Nazis in Germany, it attracted international attention. Reporters and journalists from all over the world attended the sessions. Alex Easterman, as the representative of the WJC, had a seat in full equality with members of all the Allied nations. I also met Samuel Goldsmith, a Jew from Lithuania who lived in London and, as a journalist, covered the proceedings of the trial. He subsequently visited Belsen and frequently wrote about it.

My personal feelings were a mixture of pain, anger, and satisfaction. I suffered when, as a witness, I had to identify the accused, to look at the faces of the criminals who had so sadistically mistreated us. But I also felt satisfied that some of us had survived to see them brought to justice and that for the first time the world learned about the crimes and atrocities they had committed.

I was glad the trial was over and declined the request to testify at Nuremberg. I just couldn't take part in any more "fair play" for the Nazis. At that point in my life, I couldn't understand why someone caught in flagrante committing the most brutal acts of murder and torture could possibly be found innocent, or why he would be entitled to what was considered a "fair trial." Similarly, in 1961, when the Attorney General of Israel, Dr. Gideon Hausner, asked me to appear as a witness against Adolf Eichmann, I also refused.

Soon after the Belsen Trial, Brigadier General Glyn Hughes, who had also testified for the prosecution, left Germany and returned to London. At a farewell party at military headquarters in Bad Oeynhausen, he presented me with a certificate of recognition for my work in the hospital. He also invited me to come to England,

---

5. *Trial of Josef Kramer and Forty-Four Others* (The Belsen Trial), ed. Raymond Phillips (London, Edinburgh, Glasgow: William Hodge and Co., Ltd., 1949), p. 607.

offering to make arrangements for me to live and work there. I was speechless. It was a unique opportunity. I thanked the general for his beautiful gesture but said that the time had not yet come for me to leave Belsen. There were still so many sick, and thousands of Jews remained in the camp. Maybe I could accept this noble offer in the future, but not now.

General Glyn Hughes remained a great friend of the *Belseners* and of our small family in particular. On the tenth anniversary of the liberation of Belsen in 1955, he went to Israel to take part in the ceremony of remembrance. When we moved to New York, he came to see us in our first real home after the war. When our son, Menachem, had his Bar Mitzvah in Israel in 1961, he came with his wife, Thelma, to share our happiness. In 1970, 25 years after he first entered Belsen, he joined us on a pilgrimage to its mass graves. We cherished his friendship until his death in 1973.

CHAPTER 10

~~~≋~~~

Belsen and Jews in the British Zone of Germany

We convened two congresses of the liberated Jews in the British zone of Germany. The first one took place in Belsen in September 1945, the second in Belsen and Bad Harzburg in 1947. We were supposed to open the first one on August 26, 1945, but the British denied us the necessary authorization. We then decided not to ask for permission anymore, and called the conference for September 29. Somehow a notice about it appeared in a London newspaper. The British, to save face, sent two officers, who offered their help in organizing the congress, and were even willing to host our guests from abroad. We thanked them but told them that we would do it all ourselves.

The first congress was not only an important event but also an unforgettable, emotional experience. It was held in a huge tent packed with thousands of people; many others stood outside. There were the survivors of Belsen, delegations from various Jewish communities and DP camps, and Jewish VIPs from abroad, including Selig Brodetzki, president of the Board of Deputies of British Jews; Sidney Silverman, Member of Parliament and Chairman of the WJC's British Section; Noah Barou and Alex Easterman of the WJC in London; Joseph Schwartz, the European Director of AJDC; and Meir Grabowski (later Argov), head of a delegation of the Jewish Brigade from Palestine, who greeted us by saying, "I am not worthy to stand before you." We also invited some representatives of the British Military Administration in our zone, and they all came, dressed in gala uniforms. Looking down from the stage, I noticed a young officer who was listening attentively to all the speeches and taking notes. I was intrigued. When the official program was over, many came up to the stage, among them this young officer. Professor Brodetzki saw him and exclaimed: "Vivian, what are you doing here?" Turning to us, he said: "This is my young friend, Vivian Herzog, son of Chief Rabbi Herzog." Captain Vivian Herzog later became Chaim Herzog, president of Israel. He always recalled his first visit to Belsen.

I spoke at the congress, touching upon two subjects. I knew that many young Jewish men who served in the British army were stationed in Germany. I told them about our children, the Jewish orphans, and suggested they come visit them and spend some time with them. As a result of my words, one of the young soldiers, Greville Janner, who subsequently became a longtime Labour Member of Parliament and president of the British Board of Deputies, organized a group that came often and celebrated Oneg Shabbat with the children.

The second subject I touched upon was a rather sad, unpleasant one. My words were directed specifically to the British delegation. We were receiving packages of clothes from Jews in England. They were sending us long evening dresses from Victorian times, and gold and silver evening shoes with very high heels and bows. I could imagine the old ladies opening their chests full of mothballs and getting rid of those items, satisfying their consciences by giving to charity. I said that we were deeply insulted. We did not want these things, and we did not want pity. We had not been born in Auschwitz or Belsen; we had had homes, families, love, education, and beautiful clothes, and we still had our pride. I made an exhibit of these ridiculous clothes in the office and invited the British delegation to see it. They did not say a word, but clearly they were shocked and ashamed.

After the congress, we received many letters from participants who came from abroad. The following is an English translation of a letter from Professor Brodetzki, written in Yiddish:[6]

> I don't think that I ever, in my whole life, felt such a spiritual uplift as I felt during the week I spent in Bergen-Belsen with the Jews and during their Congress. It was very difficult for me to decide to come to you. I did not know what to expect—how depressed and unhappy you would

6. Published in *Undzer Shtime*, no. 4, October 1945.

look. But you showed me a picture of pride in Jewish life, a picture that I will use to give more pride to the Jews in England. I was afraid that you might have lost your pride, but I never attended and I have never seen a more dignified Congress than yours. I was convinced that you would look with anger at the Jews from abroad, who did so little to save you from the Nazi murderers, but you welcomed me with love and warmth, and spoke to me seriously and openly. I was afraid of your sadness and tears, but you have mixed your tears with the smile of the Eternal Jew. I was afraid of your disappointment and hopelessness, but you have shown confidence and determination in your decisions. All the Jews in the entire world should learn from you. There may be no miracles: the more the Jew is being attacked, the more the Jew is being murdered, the more he shows immortality. You should be proud of your dignity during the terrible years of suffering, and you should be even more proud of your determination and decisiveness after the liberation. The whole world should be proud of your children in Belsen. Your young people will take a great part in the progress of our people.

One of the major achievements of the first congress was a close and lasting cooperation between Belsen and the German Jewish communities in the British zone. Western and eastern European Jews worked together in brotherly spirit. We elected a Central Committee for all the Jews in the British zone. The Belsen members of the Central Committee served simultaneously on the Belsen Committee. We moved the office to the "Round House," the former mess of the German officers. At the entry to this house, we erected a monument with an eternal light and the inscription "*Yizkor* (Remember) 6,000,000."

Our newly elected committee had three assignments: to fight for full freedom for the Jews in the DP camps and the German communities; to centralize all Jewish activities in one body until the liquidation of the Belsen DP camp; and to help build a Jewish state in Palestine. All these goals were fully implemented.

Political life in Belsen was an example of unity. Our young people, regardless of their political beliefs, formed one organization, called Nocham, with one aim: to go to Palestine. This picture changed when *shlikhim* (emissaries of the different Zionist political parties in Palestine) arrived in Belsen and started to form their own parties, but we managed to curb party strife from the beginning. Many of the Jewish leaders from Palestine did not agree with us because most of them could not understand the simple fact that party politics made no sense in Belsen.

We also started to work with the German Jewish communities. Many of their chairmen were German Jews who had come back from Theresienstadt. Some had been saved by their Christian wives, who, although they had been converted to Judaism, were still considered Christians, and thus were able to help their husbands. Among these men were Carl Katz of Bremen, who survived Theresienstadt with his wife, Marianne (a Jew), and their daughter; Moritz Goldsmith of Cologne; Heinz Solomon of Kiel; Nobert Prager of Hanover; Harry Goldstein of Hamburg, a proud member of the Social Democratic Party; Siegfried Heimberg of Dortmund, whose wife, a Christian woman, had never converted; and Julius Dreifuss of Düsseldorf. Yossel, the Polish Jew, created an extremely close and lasting bond between the eastern European Jewish DPs of Belsen and the German Jewish communities in the British zone, a relationship that did not exist anywhere else in Germany.

Before Rosh Hashanah of 1945, Yossel had received a package of some 25 prayer shawls from the Joint. At first, he hadn't known what to do with them, since there were thousands of Jews in Belsen. He then decided to give one *talit* to the head of each of the German Jewish communities in the British zone. All but one accepted eagerly. The exception was Nobert Prager of Hanover, who said he didn't need a *talit*. Yossel was surprised because Prager was one of the more religiously knowledgeable and observant among the German Jews. Prager explained that his wife had converted to Judaism during the 1920s, before they married. Like many such wives, she had refused to abandon her husband during the Nazi years and had willingly gone with him to Theresienstadt with their son, Rolf. When they were deported, her brother, who was a senior Nazi official in Hanover, took charge of their belongings, including Prager's prayer shawl, so that when he returned after the liberation, he got his *talit* back.

The Belsen Committee gave the Jewish communities in the British zone spiritual, religious, physical, and political help in fulfilling their religious and cultural functions. We supplied them with speakers for cultural programs (authors, rabbis, teachers). A leading member of the Jewish community in Cologne was Jacob Birnbaum, who was first vice-chairman and then chairman. When he first met Yossel, he said that everyone called him Jack. Yossel looked at him and asked, "Do you speak Yiddish?"

Birnbaum answered, "Yes, very well." Then Yossel said, "For me, you are Yankel," and Yankel he remained for Yossel. They were the closest of friends for almost 30 years until Jack's death in 1973.

Jack was a German Jew, born in Cologne. As a young man he belonged to the Jewish organization "Blue-White," which had a Zionist orientation. Because his parents had come from Poland, Jack was sent there in 1938 when the Nazis deported the so-called *Ostjuden,* Jews who were originally from eastern Europe. His sister was lucky enough to go to England, where she spent the war years, and she remained there afterward. Soon after the war started, Jack was sent to labor and concentration camps, including Płaszów. He was liberated in 1945 by the American army and returned to Cologne, where he established a factory for women's dresses. One day on the street Jack met Ilse, a young woman with whom he had been in love before the war. She was the daughter of a Jewish father and a German Christian mother who had converted to Judaism. They were the owners of a men's clothing factory. Their home and business were bombed, and her parents went into hiding in the ruins of their former factory. In the meantime, Ilse met and married the Spanish consul in Cologne. At her parents' urging, she went with him to Madrid, making arrangements with a former employee of their factory to look after her parents and provide them with food and other necessities. Ilse's parents survived thanks to the care of this man, and out of gratitude Jack established a tailor's shop for him after the war. After the war Ilse, who by now had a son and a daughter, came to Cologne to see her parents, and when she met Jack, they both realized that they still loved each other. She went back to Madrid and asked her husband for a divorce. He agreed on the condition that their son remain with him. Ilse then returned to Cologne with her daughter, Isabel. After Ilse's divorce became final, she and Jack married.

Yossel was often very helpful to Jack in his role as chairman of the Jewish community of Cologne. One day a serious problem arose. I have already mentioned Rabbi Zvi Helfgott (who later changed his name to the Hebrew Asaria), the head of the Belsen rabbinate who immigrated to Israel in 1948. There he married Malka, a young woman from Belgium. Their first child, a so-called blue baby, lived only a few days. They soon had another baby, who suffered the same fate. The doctors advised Malka to leave Israel for a short time, hoping that a change of climate and ambience would do her good. But it was 1952, a time of austerity in Israel, and it was almost impossible to obtain an exit visa. At that time, even though Israel did not have diplomatic relations with West Germany, the Israel government was about to open an Economic Mission in Cologne to implement the terms of a multibillion deutsche mark reparations agreement. Yossel went to Israel and arranged for Zvi to be assigned to the Mission, whose principal task was purchasing goods and raw materials. This action prompted a senior Israeli official, Dr. Giora Josephthal, to jokingly ask Yossel if the Mission needed a rabbi to make steel kosher. Jack Birnbaum then arranged for Zvi to become the Rabbi of Cologne. This arrangement worked for several years, but eventually misunderstandings and conflicts arose between Zvi and the leadership of the Cologne Jewish community. Yossel made numerous trips and hundreds of telephone calls to Cologne in an attempt to help Jack patch things up, but their efforts were in vain. The Helfgotts left Cologne, and subsequently, our friends Lola and Sigmund Fischel helped install Zvi as rabbi in Hanover. But this arrangement also failed to work out, and eventually the Helfgotts—or Asarias—returned to Israel.

Soon after the 1945 congress, the Central Committee decided that some of us should visit the other Jewish DP camps and Jewish communities throughout Germany. As Norbert Wollheim already had a small car, he, his future wife, Friedel, their friend Albert Kimmelstiel, and I went on that journey. We traveled from town to town, visiting the various communities. It was sad to see Jews in old-age homes, their communities without young people. To me it meant that there was no future. In the American zone we visited the Jewish DP camps of Feldafing and Landsberg. We went to the hospitals, one of which was in St. Ottilien, and whose director, Dr. Zalman Grinberg, was chairman of the Central Jewish Committee in Bavaria (later expanded to include the entire American zone). We visited the Gauting Hospital, where former tuberculosis patients were recovering. There I met a few men from my hometown and its surrounding area and encouraged them to come to Belsen after their release from the hospital. Some did.

We had a meeting in Munich with members of the Central Jewish Committee of Bavaria and tried to establish a relationship between our two committees. Present, in addition to Chairman Zalman Grinberg, were Samuel Gringauz, David Treger, and Itzhak Ratner. They were rather snobbish, I think because they lived in the city and were not constantly in touch with the DPs.

In Frankfurt Jack Trobe introduced us to Rabbi Judah Nadich, who was then a

Major in the United States Army and Adviser on Jewish Affairs to General Eisenhower. Today, he is Rabbi Emeritus of the Park Avenue Synagogue in New York, to which my children, my granddaughter, and I belong.

In Munich, I also met Dr. Paul Wiederman, my former school principal, who came to see me and brought the manuscript of his book, *Plowa Bestia (The Colorless Beast),* in which he wrote about the Judenrat in Sosnowiec. He asked for my help in getting his book translated into English. I was flattered by this request from my former principal, but as far as I know, the book appeared only in Polish.

During my travels in the American zone, I missed, to my great regret, the visit of David Ben-Gurion to Belsen in November 1945. In his speech, he said prophetically, "You see my gray hair? These gray hairs will live to see a Jewish State in Israel." In Belsen, Ben-Gurion observed Yossel in his work—his way of talking to people, his love for children—and liked what he saw. He became a friend and, years later, we often saw him and his wife, Paula, in Israel.

Ben-Gurion's visit greatly influenced our young people, who decided to go to Palestine, no matter how. Because the British still did not allow Jews to enter Palestine, they had to go on illegal emigrations, called Aliyah Bet. Some of them established a sort of kibbutz in Germany, on the border of the British and American zones, to prepare themselves for life in Palestine. This group ultimately emigrated illegally and established their kibbutz in Palestine. It was first called Kibbutz Buchenwald and later changed its name to Kibbutz Nezer Sereni.

In December 1945, Yossel was invited by Dr. Joseph Schwartz and Edward Warburg of the AJDC to attend the first postwar conference of the United Jewish Appeal (UJA) in the United States and represent the survivors to American Jewry. At first the military authorities in the British zone refused to grant him an exit permit. Then they advised him that he could go on condition that he not return to Germany. But he went and came back, and there were no repercussions.

The conference, which opened on December 15, 1945, in Atlantic City, was attended by Chaim Weizmann, president of the Jewish Agency and the World Zionist Organization; Rabbi Stephen Wise, president of the World Jewish Congress; and many other Jewish leaders from Palestine and the United States. While in Atlantic City, Yossel invited Chaim Weizmann to come to Belsen, but Weizmann said, "I have nothing to give you, nothing to offer, nothing to promise—just empty words. I refuse to come to Belsen to make false prophesies."

Yossel, one of the main speakers, delivered his 80-minute address in Yiddish, with Rabbi Nadich serving as his interpreter. The audience was prepared to hear a plea for material help, but Yossel said, "I have come to bring you greetings from the Sherit ha-Pletah, the surviving remnant of European Jewry. I will tell you what happened to us and how we are today."

The audience squirmed, and the leaders of the UJA were afraid that the American Jews in the hall would not be forthcoming with contributions, but their reaction was just the opposite. Yossel's proud appearance (in the American newspapers they called him the "Jewish Lincoln") resulted in a resolution to render all possible assistance to the Jewish DPs in Germany. The amount pledged surpassed all expectations. Maurice (Moshe) Eigen, the AJDC director in Belsen, cabled me that Yossel had delivered "two amazing speeches that shook American Jews."

Yossel remained in the United States for a month, mostly in New York City. He was invited to meetings with many Jewish organizations, workers' groups, and the PEN Club. One extraordinary meeting was with 36 Yiddish writers and poets, among them the poet H. Leivick. Yossel told them about Jewish suffering during the war, about Jewish resistance and Jewish heroism, about the Jewish plight and Jewish children, and about the conditions we were confronting in Belsen, and they listened. After that meeting Leivick wrote to Yossel (in Yiddish):

> I am still under the spell of your spirit. I understand you very well, and no matter what I say, it will not be the right words. You are going back to our brothers in the camps, and we all remain here in peaceful America. There is undoubtedly a feeling of guilt among most Jews in America. Those who do not feel it, woe to them. They are not the ones by which we should measure Jewish America. There are truly no words to describe what happened to our people during the war. One thing the Accursed One did accomplish: he filled the earth with Jewish graves and our hearts with desolation. But the victory still does not belong to him. The Jew is stronger and more everlasting. Jewish courage is not shattered. That is something I see in you. And through you, I see all the others in the camps.

At another meeting, a group of Jews from Będzin who had come to America before the war gave him a copy of the Yiddish magazine *Proletarisher Gedank*

(Proletarian Thought) published on December 1, 1944. In this issue, Yossel found an article entitled "The Graves of Our Fallen Heroes and Murdered Martyrs" and 15 obituaries. One was Yossel's! After describing his Orthodox family background and how he had become an active labor Zionist, the obituary continued with the following words: "Three times the Germans deported him from Będzin to an 'unknown destination.' The first two times, he succeeded in jumping from the train and smuggling himself back into the Będzin ghetto, so as to continue with the preparations for an organized resistance. But the German killers captured him again and deported him a third time, and this time he did not return." Apparently a friend of Yossel's, Nachman Garfinkel, saw the SS men take Yossel away and conveyed the news of his capture to the underground. For many months, he said kaddish. For Yossel, this article was not only macabre but also a sad confirmation that much was known in America about the tragedy of European Jewry, despite the claims that no one knew anything.

Yossel was supposed to stay in the United States longer, but an urgent appeal came from Ben-Gurion, asking him to return to Belsen to be a witness before the Anglo-American Committee of Inquiry on Palestine, which was supposed to come to Belsen shortly. He returned to Belsen on January 14, 1946, one day before his birthday. In his luggage were 2,378 letters from Jews in America searching for relatives in the four zones of Germany and a present for me: a lipstick, my first ever!

The Anglo-American Committee of Inquiry on Palestine, chaired by Judge Hutchinson of the United States, arrived to interview the Jewish DPs of Belsen. All of them said the same thing, that they wanted to go to Palestine. When Sir John Singleton asked Yossel, "What will you do if you are not able to go to Palestine?" he answered, "Then we shall go back to Belsen, Dachau, Buchenwald, and Auschwitz, and you will bear the moral responsibility for it."

CHAPTER 11

The Children

In the meantime, a problem arose concerning our children. In October 1945, the Jewish Refugee Committee in London, supported by UNRRA, proposed that the Jewish orphans be brought from Belsen to Great Britain and placed with various Anglo-Jewish families for adoption. When we spoke about this to the oldest children, they cried. They did not want to go live with strangers or to be separated from their friends. At a meeting of our committee, the following resolution was passed: "The Jewish Central Committee decided at a meeting at Belsen on October 21, 1945, that (a) it cannot agree to the removal of the children to England; (b) it cannot permit the children who were with us in the concentration camp to be moved from *Galut* [Diaspora] to *Galut*—they must stay where they are until their aliyah; (c) it demands that the first available aliyah certificates be allocated to the children, so that they can leave the camp as soon as possible."

When our resolution reached London, the Jewish organizations there decided to send Shlomo Adler Rudel, a member of the Jewish Agency for Palestine, to Belsen to discuss the matter with us again. He arrived in December 1945, held meetings with us, spoke to the children, and returned to London. A short while later, we sent him a letter stating:

> Following our conversations about the children in the British Zone, we are sending you herewith our decision. The Central Committee reiterates its resolve not to permit the children to be taken to England but to

send them to Eretz Yisrael when the time comes. We recognize that conditions in Belsen are not good for the children. Our Committee has taken up this point with the British and received an assurance that the mansion of the Warburg family in Blankenese, near Hamburg, will be put at our disposal for a children's house. The children will be taken to Blankenese at once. We realize our responsibility in caring for the children, and we believe that everything is being done to ensure their physical and mental comfort. The establishment of the children's home at Blankenese will not, however, diminish our efforts to take them to Eretz Yisrael at the earliest opportunity.

The children were happy. Three boys went to England, and the other 98 children were transferred to the magnificent Warburg estate, together with a team of teachers and supervisors. For the first time after so many years of suffering, our children were able to enjoy a restful and comfortable existence and to continue their education. How happy and proud they were when they could play host to visitors, especially to their former schoolmates from Belsen.

In March 1946, Ruth Kluger, the representative of the Jewish Agency in Paris, brought 101 certificates for Palestine: 98 for the children and 3 for their teachers. She helped us prepare the transport. One of the brightest days for all of us was April 9, 1946, when the first transport of children left for Israel. I was privileged to accompany the children. I was helped during the trip, until we boarded the ship, by two representatives of the AJDC, Charlotte Rosenbaum of France and Sylvia Newlaender of New York. Two women from the Jewish Relief Unit and the Jewish Agency went with us to Palestine. They had all been working with the children in Blankenese. The children from the American zone were accompanied by Itzhak Ratner, a member of the Central Committee in the American zone. It was an unforgettable journey.

Unfortunately, my leaving for Palestine meant that I would be away from Belsen on April 15, the first anniversary of our liberation in Belsen. I knew that there would be a ceremony at the site of the mass graves and that a Jewish monument would be erected there. The inscription on the stone read, "Israel and the world shall remember the 30,000 Jews exterminated in the concentration camp Bergen-Belsen at the hands of the murderous Nazis. Earth conceal not the blood shed on thee."

We boarded the train in Hanover for Marseille, where the *Champollion* was waiting for us. When our train stopped in Lyon, a delegation of local Jews appeared on the platform and greeted us with bread and salt. They cried unashamedly, looking at the Jewish children. We spent a few days in the camp of former Yugoslav POWs and celebrated the first seder in the open, under the skies. It was a festive and joyous evening. Our children were wonderful. They peeled potatoes, decorated the tables, and distributed the matzos we had received from the AJDC. They were ecstatic to feel like the hosts.

While in Marseille, we met a Jewish family from Tunisia, a husband, wife, and two babies. We were told that two of their sons were already in Palestine, where they had joined the Haganah (the underground Jewish army in Palestine). They begged us to take them with us. I had a hard time with the husband, who spoke Arabic and French. When they boarded the ship, I told him that he and his wife were traveling under the respective names of two youngsters from the American zone who had been unable to come because they had come down with measles. I wrote the names on a piece of paper for him, but every few hours he would come to me and ask, *"Comment je m'appelle?"* (What's my name?) After trying repeatedly to explain the situation and the need for caution, I told him that he should not speak when any authorities were around. But this seemed to make no impression on him. When we arrived at Haifa, while I was presenting the list of our children to a British officer, the Tunisian came up to me and, in front of the officer, asked the usual question: *"Comment je m'appelle?"* I froze. Luckily, the British officer either didn't understand French or didn't pay attention. I excused myself, telling the officer that the man needed some urgent help. I handed the list to one of the older girls and asked her to continue. I then went over to three young Jewish men who worked with the Aliyah Bet (the illegal immigration to Palestine) and had boarded the ship shortly before we reached Haifa and told them to somehow get the Tunisian couple off the ship before the man caused a real catastrophe. They did so. I returned to finish the roll call, and nothing else happened.

There were also two expectant mothers whose husbands were already at sea trying to reach Palestine illegally. They were also promised that they could come with us. The evening before we were to board the *Champollion,* one of the women began to have labor pains and was rushed to the hospital in Marseille. The following morning I went to see her, but the baby had not come yet. I explained the situation to the French doctor, begging him to arrange to have the woman returned to the ship if the baby was not born by noon. The doctor agreed. She returned to the ship before we left port. On the first day at sea, we received an additional passenger; her baby boy was born, with the aid of the ship's doctor. Two days later, the other woman gave birth to a little girl. Our older girls were wonderful. They helped the mothers take care of the babies.

Our ship stopped in Bizerte, Tunisia, on a Friday. A delegation of local Jews, headed by their rabbi, came aboard to greet us. The rabbi appeared in his festive robe, a white aba, and a red yarmulke. He gave us wine and his blessings. The Jewish children of Bizerte, all boys, marched on board, carrying crates of oranges on their heads in Oriental fashion. We were deeply moved.

We arrived in Haifa on Thursday, April 26, 1946, and were received like long-lost brothers and sisters, as, in fact, we were. A delegation of women came to welcome us, among them Vera Weizmann, the wife of Israel's first President, Chaim Weizmann. The two babies and their mothers were taken immediately to the hospital.

Because we had illegal immigrants with us and did not yet know where our children would be sent, we went voluntarily to Atlit, the clearing camp for new immigrants to Palestine. The camp was guarded by British special policemen, and the children were frightened when they saw them. The day after our arrival, members of all political parties in Palestine came to see the children. On Sunday morning, without consulting the teachers or me, they started to interview the children. I learned this accidentally when Brachah, a 15-year-old girl from Hungary, came to me crying. She told me that she was asked questions about her parents—whether her mother lit candles on Friday night, if their store was open on the Sabbath. She was told that they wanted to send her to a religious kibbutz. Furious, I opened the door of the barrack where the interrogators were sitting. I introduced myself again, although they had met me a day earlier, and expressed my dismay and disappointment over their actions. I told them that the party "key," as they called it, should be applied to material objects, not to our children. I reminded them that these children had spent their childhood in ghettos and concentration camps. They were orphans; they had nobody in the world except the friends with whom they were staying now; and they wanted to remain together. If there was no place for all of them in one kibbutz, they should be allowed to form groups of friends with whom they wanted to stay. Fortunately, I succeeded. We ended up dividing the children into three groups. Eighteen of the youngest went to Ben-Shemen, where the principal of the school was Arieh Simon, a former member of the Jewish Brigade, who had taught the children in Blankenese and knew them well. I said to the other 80, "Look, you can't all remain together. But you are not all friends with one another. Friends should keep together. Divide yourselves into two groups, 40 and 40, and group yourselves with your friends. I am not going to influence you. You have to do this yourselves." So they made their own decision; 40 of them went to Kibbutz Kiryat Anavim outside of Jerusalem, and the other 40 to Kibbutz Dorot. The procedures took a whole week and ended on a Thursday. The children left for their assigned destinations, and I went to Tel Aviv.

On Friday, I visited the children in Kiryat Anavim and saw that they were treated with love and affection. That night, as we were sitting at the Sabbath meal, I knew that our children had at last come home. I also visited the children in Ben-Shemen and Dorot, and saw that they were happy. There was no problem of absorption, as our children had been prepared for Palestine in our Belsen school. They knew Hebrew very well and easily became part of the Yishuv. They soon became free and proud citizens of the State of Israel.

I remained in Palestine for four weeks. I met my friends who had gone there before the war as well as many important leading personalities. I will never forget my visit to the home of Dr. Chaim Weizmann in Rehovoth. He had heard about the children from his wife and called on the Saturday after my arrival to invite me for lunch, sending his car to pick me up. After lunch Dr. Weizmann sat with me and asked many questions. He walked with me in his beautiful garden asking even more. Finally he brought me into a room that looked like a mausoleum. There were books, relics, and photos of his son, who had been killed in the war, and I had the feeling that he wanted me to know that he also suffered.

The following day I met with four of my former classmates who had been lucky enough to have come to Palestine before the war. They invited others from our hometown, and we sat for hours, recollecting our young, happy years. They gave me pictures of our classes and school. I was also moved by the surprise party given for me by the members of the Jewish Brigade who had visited us and worked with us in Belsen.

On May 14, I was invited to attend a plenary session of the Va'ad Le'umi, the temporary Jewish parliament, to speak about Belsen. After I finished, David Remez, co-chairman of the Va'ad Le'umi, announced the plans to establish Yad Vashem, a national memorial authority for the annihilated Jews of Europe. The Jews in Belsen and in the British zone were among the first to contribute to this institution. At the home of David Remez I met many prominent personalities of the Zionist political establishment. Again, there were questions, which I answered very politely. I understood their curiosity, but I could never tolerate questions about our psychological condition. At one point, I rebelled. Among the guests was Golda Meir, at that time Goldie Meyerson, who asked how many abnormal people there were in Belsen. I looked at her and answered, "We are all abnormal because we remained normal." She swallowed my answer and for years, whenever we met, she would say, "Hadassah, you taught me a good lesson."

Thanks to the generosity of the Jewish Agency, I had the use of a car and a guide to show me around, so I went to Jerusalem, to the Western Wall, and prayed. I said kaddish and cried. I also went to the Kibbutz Tel Itzhak, which was established by young people from my own hometown. It is a kibbutz of Ha-No'ar ha-Tsioni, the general Zionist movement, to which my brother and I had belonged. Most important, they gave me a photograph of my brother Yumek, together with other members of the underground movement in our ghetto.

After all the visits, I said good-bye to my friends and left. On June 6, I boarded the ship *André LeBon* for Marseille. I was hoping to have a restful trip because I was exhausted, but it was wishful thinking. The ship was overcrowded. In addition to the 1,000 passengers already on board, the ship had to go to Lebanon and take 1,000 French army personnel back to France. A French couple was added to each cabin. The situation was not very pleasant, and I felt extremely uncomfortable. On the ship I met two young Jewish girls from Palestine who were going to Sweden to work for the Jewish Agency for Palestine. They felt the same way I did, so I came up with an idea. There was a huge empty room in which there was a grand piano, a concert hall of sorts. I asked the captain to allow the three of us to sleep there on the floor, covered with a carpet. I had endured far worse. The captain was amused, but he gave his permission for this unusual arrangement.

When I arrived in Marseille, I did not know how I would get to Belsen. My trip on the *Champollion,* the five weeks in Palestine, and the weeklong journey on the *André LeBon* had left me physically and mentally exhausted. As I was standing in line on the deck to go through passport control, I felt that somebody was looking at me from the side. Annoyed—I felt that I needed unwanted attention like a *lokh in kop* (Yiddish for a hole in the head)—I turned to see who the person was and almost screamed. There was Yossel. He had come especially from Belsen to meet me. He had managed to get on deck of the ship, and although he didn't know a word of French, had found a French policeman who took me out of the line, cleared my papers, and arranged for a porter to take my suitcase. We had a room in a hotel with a bathtub, hot running water, and a little fruit. I thought I was in paradise.

We went back to Belsen via Paris and decided to go to a movie. When we realized that we were seeing a documentary about Hitler, we started laughing, left the theater, and went back to the hotel. The following day we took a train back to Belsen.

We were married on August 18, 1946. We did not marry sooner, although we lived together, as did many other couples in Belsen. There were two reasons: one was religious—a certain period of time had to pass to confirm the death of our previous mates; the second was that we just wanted to know each other better. At first, after the liberation, I had lived in the hospital in Block 55 to be near the patients. And then one day, I think it was in June, Major Johnston and another British doctor arrived with some furniture—a chair, a sofa, and a table—and said it was time I had a nice home. They went to a block called *Kantine* 2, furnished a room for me, and I moved in. One evening not too long after that, Yossel took me home, came up to the room with me, and stayed. It was as simple as that.

Often at the beginning, when couples came to Yossel and told him that they were about to get married, he advised them to wait, to make sure they were marrying for the right reasons, out of love, in order to create a new family together. If, however, they wanted to be together because they were lonely after the years of hell we had all endured, he said that they should just live together for a while to see if the relationship was real and would last.

Our wedding took place in Lübeck in the home of our friends Friedel and Norbert Wollheim. Our friend Rabbi Zvi Helfgott performed the ceremony. Because we wanted to avoid a spectacle in Belsen, only a few of our closest friends were present. The following month we received a letter from David Ben-Gurion, congratulating us. Translated from the Yiddish, it reads:

Paris, September 2, 1946

To the dear and respected Hadassah and Josef Rosensaft

Dear *Haverim* and Friends,

Ruth Kluger just told me the joyful news about your wedding. Please accept my heartfelt and brotherly *mazel-tov*. Such an event is always full of joy, and in this case for me personally and I believe for many of your friends as well, an outstanding happy occasion.

My visit in Belsen was for me one of the deepest experiences, not only tragic, but the memories were encouraging and comforting, especially having met Yossel Rosensaft. I saw before me a real, prominent confirmation of Jewish vitality and idealism, the two virtues that prevailed in the long and bitter Diaspora. Alas, I did not meet Hadassah in Belsen, but from what I heard from everybody about her and even the spirit that I felt when people were talking about her, I thought that she is the second and maybe even the first "Yossel," but not so dictatorial as he. And then destiny brought you together. It is a symbol that fate is not so terrible but is a little bit, although seldom, decent, because it could not have made a better union. And so, be happy in your new bond; happy as you and your peers deserve; happy in your deep love; happy to create a new family; happy in your commitment to your unfortunate people that will surely live in liberty and independence in its own land and in its own state.

Some couples went on their honeymoon in the mountains in Germany, but we just couldn't bring ourselves to do that.

CHAPTER 12

Belsen: 1946–1950

O nce Yossel and I were married, I wanted to resign from the Central Committee because I felt it was not appropriate for a husband and wife to serve together, but the other members refused to accept my resignation. They said that I had not been elected to the committee because of Yossel, but on my own merit, and that I should stay on my own merit. So I remained and worked.

At the second congress of the Jewish DPs in the British zone, in July 1947, I was asked by the heads of the German Jewish communities to become the chairman of their new Council. I thanked them for their vote of confidence but said that the chairman should be a German Jew. I proposed Carl Katz, a capable, reasonable man. They elected him on condition that I would agree to be vice-chairman, which I did.

At the 1947 congress, I submitted the following report on the activities of the Central Committee's Health Department since October 1945:

> The Central Committee has succeeded, after many endeavours, in taking over the Health Services of the Jewish Communities and Committees in the British Zone. Since then the Health Committee of the Central Committee in Bergen-Belsen has been the headquarters and advisory body for all existing Jewish ambulances and health institutions in the British Zone. All committees and communities have submitted to the health department detailed reports as to the general state of health of

their members. To recount all that has been done by the department would be too lengthy—we will merely give the data from the reports in hand.

The average sickness rate among our Jewish people in the British Zone does not exceed 7 percent—this is very satisfactory.

We receive constant and recurring complaints from the Jewish institutions in the following vein: "Give us Jewish doctors and nurses so that we do not have to consult German doctors and enter German hospitals where we feel unhappy and strange." This demand, which is certainly justified, has unfortunately not been able to be fulfilled up to now, the reason being the lack of Jewish doctors and nursing staff. Our endeavours with the American Joint Distribution Committee and Jewish Relief Unit have up to now had no results.

It must be noted that the position in the camp Bergen-Belsen is completely different from that in the whole of the British Zone. Here we have an independent self-administration; this directs all camp institutions—the whole apparatus of the health service lying in Jewish hands.

Since August 1946, the hospital has been made available to Jewish patients only; these are supported by the Committee. We already have the provisional agreement that in the near future this hospital in Belsen will be open to all the Jews in the British Zone. This would enable us to have all our sick under one center of medical control, receiving our cooperation. Today the situation is as follows: for example, in Hamburg there are 38 Jews sick in various hospitals and institutions; in Hannover there are 15 Jews sick in 9 different hospitals. The statistics show that there is in Belsen a proportionately larger number of sick than in the other provinces. A true estimation of the state of health in this camp can be obtained from the work in the Out-Patient department. For the year ending January 1946 there were 13,600 sick treated; for the year ending January 1947 the number increased to 15,000. This was due to the arrival of refugees from Russia.

Of interest is the fact that a number of cases who had complained to the doctors of trivial complaints such as headaches and colds were found, after a thorough examination, to be suffering from tuberculosis. Following on this, it was thought advisable to have chest X-rays of all

Jewish inhabitants of the British Zone. This was accordingly done, the majority of the people submitting to this measure. The health department has established in the Belsen hospital a department for children suffering from tuberculosis; here, young people and children from Bergen-Belsen and 13 communities were brought; of these people we have been able, thanks to the A.J.D.C. and the J.R.U. to send to date 79 people to Switzerland (Davos) and 48 to Italy (Merano: to sanatoria under Joint and Relief auspices). From letters received from patients we feel that their condition improves from week to week. A number of patients have already returned cured and it is to be hoped that we will shortly be able to send other patients to these vacant beds. Other tuberculosis patients under treatment in hospitals or Out-Patient clinics are being supported by the Central Committee, the Joint, and the Relief both medically and materially as far as possible.

All other cases of sickness are a result either of concentration camp life or the war. In many people the sad experiences undergone have left deep scars. Of special event in the life of the Sherit ha-Pletah are the newborn children. 650 infants were born during the last 10 months; their state of health is satisfactory but the lack of Jewish pediatricians is felt; it is easy to understand that a Jewish mother has little desire to entrust her child to a German doctor.

The dental department plays an important role in the health service. During the war, and concentration camp years, there was little opportunity for our people to have dental treatment and as a result these were in very bad condition; to date 18,500 dental cases have received treatment. The establishment of a dental laboratory proved to be necessary; one was established under the able assistance of Greenman (O.R.T.) and has since its beginning made 383 sets of artificial teeth. The laboratory is at the disposal of all Jews in the British Zone and especially to those who are about to emigrate to Palestine.

Mention should be made here of the Convalescent Homes. After six years of war our Jewish people are all exhausted and need a special kind of relaxation; the tasks which the convalescent homes have taken over are therefore of a special significance. The convalescent home in Bad

Harzburg offers to 120 people every month rest, relaxation, and all possible help. This home is under the supervision of a committee consisting of Dr. Bimko, Carl Katz, and the directors of the Joint and Relief. The administration is done by Samuel Klein, who fulfills his duties with great conscientiousness. Up to date 935 people have had a period of relaxation and convalescence in this home.

Another home for children up to 12 years has been established in Blankenese; 100 children are accommodated at a time for a period of 4–6 weeks. In Lüneburg there is another home taking 30 children at a time; this home is especially run on strictly religious lines and took in for the most part children from religious families. In Belsen, a home for child orphans has been established; here, too, children whose mothers are in hospital or convalescent homes can be accommodated.

It must be stated, however, that in the sphere of health service much more could have been achieved than has in fact been done. The big difficulties such as lack of doctors, nursing staff and specialists (e.g. children's specialists, surgeons, and psychiatrists) were not able to be surmounted. There is hope that the new promises made by the A.J.D.C. and the J.R.U. will be fulfilled in the near future.

This report cannot close without specially stressing the fact that what has been accomplished is largely due to the workers of the Jewish Voluntary Services, the American Joint Distribution Committee and the Jewish Relief Unit.

We also wish to stress the excellent help and cooperation which the health department received from the medical supervisor of the Joint, Dr. Spanier.

During our years in Belsen, we also took part in international Jewish and Zionist meetings. When I became a Zionist as a teenager, I read about Theodor Herzl, the founder of modern Zionism, and about the first Zionist Congress, held in Basel. I never dreamed that I would one day attend such a conference. The first postwar Zionist Congress took place in December 1946, also in Basel. Belsen had its own delegation, including, in addition to Yossel and myself, Berl Laufer, Samuel Weintraub, Shmayahu (later Sam) Bloch, Romek Zynger, Raphael Olewski, and David

Rosenthal. I was deeply disappointed by the congress. The Jewish martyrs were eulogized only once, by Zalman Rubashow (Shazar), who later became the third president of Israel. That was all the time the Zionist leaders devoted to the destruction of European Jewry. Most of the congress was devoted to an ugly fight for power. The American delegation, led by Rabbi Abba Hillel Silver, succeeded in removing Dr. Chaim Weizmann as president of the World Zionist Organization. I was saddened because I was a supporter and admirer of Dr. Weizmann, and I was disgusted by the infighting and political greed.

Yossel was also elected to the European Executive of the World Jewish Congress, representing the Jews of Belsen and of the British zone. In April 1947, he took part in that body's meeting in Prague. Jan Masaryk, the foreign minister of Czechoslovakia, greeted the delegation cordially but was very pessimistic about the political future of his country. Then the participants went to Theresienstadt, where part of our Jewish tragedy had been enacted. After that they went to Lidice, the site of a Czech village that had been destroyed by the Nazis in 1942 in retaliation for the assassination of Reinhard Heydrich, the Deputy Reichsprotektor of Moravia and Bohemia. There, Yossel was asked to speak.

In July 1948, our Central Committee was represented at the WJC's General Assembly in Montreux, Switzerland, by Yossel, Harry Goldstein, Norbert Wollheim, Berl Laufer, Samuel Weintraub, and David Rosenthal. There Yossel got to know Dr. Nahum Goldmann, who had been one of the founders of the World Jewish Congress together with Rabbi Stephen S. Wise, and who would succeed Rabbi Wise as its president the following year. Dr. Goldmann and Yossel developed a good relationship that later became a friendship between our families.

After I returned from Palestine in June 1946, there were still 200 Jewish orphans in Belsen and Lüneburg who had been brought to us toward the end of 1945 from Russia and eastern Europe, where their parents had perished. We took care of them, housing them in Blocks RB5 and RB6 (where the first group of children had lived before they were taken to the Warburg mansion in Blankenese). It was our intention that these children would also eventually go to Palestine.

In the early spring of 1947, we had a visit from Mrs. Regina Boritzer of Zurich, who came on behalf of a Jewish women's organization in Switzerland. The women offered to give some of the older children a nice summer vacation in their homes. Each of several Swiss families was willing to take in one child. I told the children about the invitation and asked if any of them wanted to go. About 50 of them agreed, so in June, Vida Kaufman of the AJDC and I took them to Basel. We arrived in the early evening and were welcomed by a few Swiss Jewish ladies. The children were put to bed in a big hall at the railroad station, and Vida and I stayed in a little room nearby.

At about 10 p.m., we heard noises and crying from the children's room. We rushed in to find a real uproar. Two of the Swiss women had decided to talk to the children (who understood very little German) and start a "selection" of who would go where and to which families. Furious, I asked them why they had not consulted me, and why they had come so late in the evening, when the children were supposed to be asleep.

Suddenly, I noticed that two children, a sister and brother, were missing. Rose was 12 years old and Yossi was 10. Nobody knew where they had gone. I learned from one of the older children that the women had told them that each Swiss family would take only one child, so Rose and Yossi would not be able to stay together. Rose had promised her dying mother that she would take care of Yossi and never leave him. I ran out to the nearest platform. A train was standing there. (Luckily, local trains did not run in Switzerland at night.) I looked through the windows of the compartments and finally spotted the children sitting in a corner, glued to each other and scared. I took them out, comforted them, and promised them that they would stay with me.

I went back and told the Swiss women that I appreciated their charitable gesture, but they were greatly mistaken if they expected these children to be like the children they knew, with good manners, children who say "thank you" and "please," who fold napkins after a meal, who sit quietly at the dinner table eating with a knife and fork. These were orphans who had seen their parents killed, who had grown up without a home, without love, and often without enough food. They would only be unhappy staying with Swiss families, and I was going to take them back to Belsen.

The atmosphere was tense. Then, Regina Boritzer arrived and had an idea. She contacted a young man who managed a training center for young people who wanted to go to Palestine. It was located on a farm in the Alps, above St. Gallen, and was empty at that time. The young man came over, spoke to the children, and they liked the idea of going there, especially since they were promised that they could all stay together. The children spent three weeks on the farm and then returned to us in Belsen.

In March 1947, the British announced that Belsen would receive 400 aliyah certificates monthly. These were allocated solely for Belsen, but we believed that it was our duty to share them with other Jews in Germany, which we did. We still had to get certificates for the children. Yossel decided to go to London to see Foreign Minister Ernest Bevin to ask for 200 certificates for the children over and above the monthly Belsen quota. Nobody believed his mission could be successful, especially since at the time bloody fights were taking place in Palestine between the British and the Jews. Even leaders of the Jewish Agency for Palestine and the World Jewish Congress tried to discourage him from meeting with Bevin. Yossel replied, "I can't lose because I have nothing to lose. Whatever I get, I will get. I have no army. I am not going to war. I am not going to fight. They can't be afraid of me. I am only going to ask. I don't risk anything. They can only say no, but I have to try." So he went. Colonel Robert Solomon, the Jewish Adviser to the Control Office for Germany and Austria, arranged for Yossel to see Bevin. Solomon later told us that Yossel said, "Mr. Foreign Minister, your army liberated us, and we are grateful. We'll never forget it. But now you have to let us live. These orphaned children want to go to Palestine. Help them." On the spot, Yossel obtained the extra 200 certificates for the children.

The children left for Palestine in 1947. The British authorities made a Red Cross train available for them with all the facilities, plenty of food, and even a kosher kitchen. Senior officers of the British military government, General Fenshaw and Brigadier General Kenchington, came to see them off. After their arrival in Palestine, the children were cared for by the Youth Aliyah, especially by David Umansky, with whom I had worked closely previously. Most of the children were taken in by Jewish families.

In May 1947, four young Jewish members of the Etzel, the Revisionist underground movement in Palestine headed by Menachem Begin, came from the American zone to Hanover, in the British zone, hoping to dynamite railroad tracks and blow up a train loaded with British soldiers as an act of protest against the British policies in Palestine. They were caught before any explosion could occur and were sentenced to death by a British military court at Hanover. Begin sent an emissary to Belsen to ask Yossel for his help. Yossel again went to London and, with the help of the

World Jewish Congress, met with senior British government officials, including Bevin, to urge that the death sentences be commuted. Asked if he thought the four youths were innocent, Yossel said no, he didn't think that. He was then asked if he thought that the trial had been unfair, and he replied that he didn't think that either. He was then asked if there were any mitigating circumstances he could think of, and he said he did not know of any. In that case, Yossel was asked, on what possible basis was he asking for the four death sentences to be commuted? He replied, "We, the Jews in Belsen, will not allow any of our fellow Jews to be executed in Germany. If you want to execute these four boys, you can take them to England!" Yossel knew that, legally, the men could not be transferred out of Germany for execution. Thanks to his efforts, two of the men were released and the other two resentenced to 20 years' imprisonment.

This episode had an interesting postscript. After the establishment of the State of Israel in May 1948, the British government released all Jewish political prisoners (mostly members of the Etzel and Lehi underground movements) who were interned in various parts of the world—except for the two Etzel men, Abraham Hubert and Jacob Redlich, who remained in a British military prison in Werl, Germany. Again, Begin asked Yossel to intervene, and again Yossel went to London. When he raised the subject with the British authorities, he was asked whether anyone had formally asked for their release. Embarrassed, Yossel discovered that the Israelis had failed to do so. He was told that the two prisoners would be released upon a formal application, on condition that they leave Germany within 24 hours. The application was duly made, and on May 4, 1950, Hubert and Redlich left Germany for Israel.

The happiest day in Yossel's and my life was May 1, 1948, the day of the birth of our son in Belsen. We named him Menachem Zwi, after our two fathers, but for us and our friends, he was "Meni" from the beginning. A little being with big blue eyes and blond hair, he filled our hearts with joy and gratitude. Our outspoken neighbor in *Kantine* 2, Clara Silbernik, would often knock at our door and ask why our baby was so quiet, why he hardly ever seemed to cry. I explained to her that if a baby is healthy, dry, and not hungry, there is no reason for him to cry.

More than 2,000 babies were born in the Belsen DP camp, and each was a gift from God. I always felt it a great miracle that we women, after having gone through so much suffering, were still able to give birth. At times the joy was doubled, as when, on July 14, 1946, the first of several sets of twins born in Belsen—Jaffa and Itzhak, the children of our friends Eva and Romek Zynger—arrived.

Because of the various illnesses to which I had been exposed in Birkenau and Belsen, my pregnancy was a difficult one. Dr. Noah Barou, Ruth Shaerf, and other British friends urged me repeatedly to come to London before our child was due and have the delivery in a hospital there. I was grateful for their concern but declined. How could I, a member of the Central Committee and the wife of its chairman, take advantage of such an opportunity while all the other Jewish women in Belsen had to have their babies in the DP camp's hospital, with German doctors in attendance? It would have suggested that I considered myself more privileged than the others or, even worse, that I did not have confidence in these doctors. I simply could not do this. In the end, our son was born healthy and strong, albeit after a long labor. Yossel waited to see him, and then went to lead the annual May Day parade through Belsen.

Shortly after Meni was born, Noah Barou called from London to ask us which school we wanted our son to attend. Apparently, it was the English custom to enroll children in prestigious schools at birth, and Dr. Barou wanted to arrange this for Meni. We thanked him for his thoughtfulness but told him that we did not think we would settle in England.

Two weeks after Meni's birth, on May 15, 1948, the State of Israel was proclaimed by David Ben-Gurion. We used to say jokingly that this was the greatest birthday present our Meni received. The creation of a Jewish state was a kind of compensation for our suffering. We knew very well that had a Jewish state existed before the war, millions of Jews could have been saved.

Young men from Belsen went to Israel under assumed names to join the new Israeli army and fight in Israel's War of Independence. They were taken directly from the boat to the battlefront. Many of them were killed. Despite our own hardships, the *Belseners* sent tons of food, thousands of pairs of boots, blankets, hospital equipment, money, and machinery for Israel's first gunpowder factory to help in this war.

In the spring of 1949, Yossel and I were in Paris with Norbert and Friedel Wollheim and Max and Clara Silbernik. One day I took the other women on a walking tour of Paris. We were nearing the Opera House when suddenly a man hugged and kissed me. I was stunned, as were my friends. When I looked at the man, I almost screamed. There was Mundek Frey, my friend and colleague from my student years in Nancy. The plan of showing my friends Paris was over. I sat with Mundek in a coffeehouse for hours, listening to his war experiences—how he had escaped from Paris to the United States. Mundek then worked for some time with Dr. Albert Schweitzer in Africa and ultimately settled in Manhattan, where he opened a practice. Many years later, he became our family's dentist.

In April 1949, Yossel was invited to visit Israel. He went with Norbert Wollheim and Sigmund Fischel from Hanover. Yossel was received very well, had meetings with members of the government and the Jewish Agency for Palestine, and saw his friends. At the same time, a transport with many Jews from Belsen arrived, and he went to Haifa harbor to see them. He knew that the newcomers were being sent to transit camps, including one called Pardés Hanna (*pardes* means orchard in Hebrew). He and Norbert went there and found terrible living conditions. Belsen families who had arrived earlier were living in water-logged huts. Because Norbert wore a French beret and carried a camera, people thought that he was a journalist and showed him sick children covered with furuncles. Heavy rain almost flooded the camp. Yossel was furious that not a single family in Israel offered to take in even one child for protection from the storm.

He went back to Jerusalem, had meetings with members of the Cabinet, and asked them how they could sleep while children in the transit camps were forced to live in deep, cold water. He met with Giora Josephthal, head of the absorption department of the Jewish Agency, and asked the same question. Dr. Josephthal, a German Jew, told him that one day a delegation of *Belseners* staying in Pardés Hanna came to see him and asked to be transferred to Pardés Yossel. Josephthal searched the map of Israel for Pardés Yossel but could not find any such place. Then the delegation told him that they wanted to go back to Belsen, to Yossel. This experience had such an impact on Yossel that he decided he could not live in Israel, even though I had already made plans to work in Israel and we had sent a fully equipped dental cabinet there. We never retrieved that dental equipment from the port in Haifa.

After his return from Israel, Yossel delivered a powerful speech to the Jews of Belsen. He told them that Israel was a wonderful but difficult country and urged them to make aliyah (that is, to go to Israel), as long as they were prepared for the harsh conditions they would encounter there. He also told them that they would be on their own. "Ben-Gurion will not meet you at the boat," he said, "and Eliezer Kaplan [Israel's first finance minister] will not present you with a check."

Yossel remained a devoted Zionist, made significant contributions to Israel, and helped the state in many situations. Over time, he supported many institutions and organizations: the Israel Museum in Jerusalem, to which he gave two Chagall paintings; the Hebrew University; various hospitals; the Weizmann Institute, where he was a member of its board of governors; and several children's funds.

In July 1949, an emissary from Ben-Gurion, a man named Robinson, came to see Yossel with a special message from the prime minister. There was a German gunpowder factory in the American zone. One night some Israelis took the machines out through the roof and put them in a wagon to send them to a port and on to Israel. The Americans discovered what had happened and tried to find the stolen machinery. Ben-Gurion asked Yossel for help in order to avoid political and other consequences. Yossel's idea was to have the machinery brought to Bergen, in the vicinity of Belsen. The Israelis agreed, and Yossel bribed the German customs officers so that the machinery reached the Bergen railroad station. There the machinery remained until a way was found to send it to Israel.

Someone then had the idea to put the shipment on the *Dromit,* an Israeli ship, as soon as it arrived in Germany, and the equipment was taken to Bremen. In the meantime, Yossel was supposed to go to London for a meeting. He woke me in the middle of one night, saying that he would not go to London until the machinery was secured and had decided not to wait for the *Dromit.* The following morning he went to Bremen, to the Neuhaus firm, which handled the transport of our people's belongings to Israel. He asked Neuhaus to hire a small boat, put the machines on it, and send them to Israel. This was done. Once the boat was in international waters, the cargo was safe, and in due course it reached Israel.

In August 1949, the *Dromit* was about to leave Bremen for Israel carrying the possessions of 155 DP families, most of them from Belsen, who were emigrating. In addition to their personal belongings, the cargo contained 680 packing cases consisting of equipment, tools, and materials that would enable the newcomers to earn their livelihood in Israel. Just as the ship was due to leave the harbor, the American authorities stopped it from sailing, saying that the cargo of the Jewish DPs was illegal. They were looking for the machinery for the gunpowder factory (that had already been sent to Israel), and they looked for contraband arms.

All this happened while Yossel was in London. He immediately returned to Bremen, where he pleaded with the Israeli captain not to unload the goods because as long as they were on the boat they belonged to the nation of the ship's registry. The captain refused his request: the cargo was unloaded and searched, but nothing was found. Because the property in question had originated in the British zone, the American authorities transferred the whole matter to the British authorities, who confiscated the entire cargo and started intensive investigations. They threatened to prosecute Yossel as the one responsible for shipping allegedly illegal goods to Israel. Our legal adviser, Dr. Hendrik Van Dam, tried to comfort me by saying he was certain that Yossel would not be sentenced to more than five years in prison. Some consolation! It took a whole year of proceedings and interventions. We engaged a London barrister who made several trips to Germany to conduct inquiries on the spot. Representations were made by the World Jewish Congress to the highest British authorities. Finally, the cargo was released, and all the charges against Yossel were dropped. It then turned out that much of the seized cargo had spoiled, especially food that people had taken along with them. We received compensation from the British for these items and for our expenses. We bought fresh food with this money and sent it to the Youth Aliyah in Israel for distribution there.

At the beginning of 1950, we heard that Berl Laufer, the former secretary of the Central Jewish Committee, who had immigrated to Israel in 1949 with his wife and their little boy, had a serious problem. His wife was suffering from a severe skin disease, and the doctors said the climate in Israel was killing her. Berl had been an ardent and active Zionist since his youth and didn't know what to do. At Yossel's urging, the family returned to Belsen and made plans to leave as soon as possible for Canada. The problem was: Who would pay for his passage there, and how could he regain his DP status and receive his emigration subsidy, since his previous trip to Israel had already been paid for. Yossel consulted Dr. Joseph Schwartz of the AJDC in Paris, who promised to help. After a heated debate at a meeting of the Jewish Agency in Paris, Laufer received his clearance and was able to go to Canada.

On September 6, 1950, the Belsen DP camp was closed. All but a handful of its former inhabitants had left Germany for Israel, the United States, Canada, Australia, and elsewhere. A special ceremony and meeting was held in the Round House, the headquarters of the Central Jewish Committee. It was attended by *Belseners;* members of Jewish communities in Germany; local British officials; and representatives of the British government, the State of Israel, the AJDC, the IRO, and the WJC. First we marched to the mass graves to pray and remember our martyrs. Yossel gave a moving account of the history of the Jewish DP organization and our struggle for survival over the last five and a half years. He paid tribute to the aid provided by the British liberating army and especially its medical services under the leadership of Brigadier General Glyn Hughes. With this ceremony the chapter of the Jewish DPs in the British zone was closed.

Bergen-Belsen has two different meanings for those who were there before and after the liberation. We not only remember Belsen as a symbol of man's inhumanity to man, but we also remember Belsen after the liberation as a place that became the symbol of rehabilitation, both physical and spiritual, of Jewish survivors, an example of organized Jewish self-help and political activity, and the scene of a successful struggle for Jewish rights. As Yossel once explained:

> Belsen was a Jewish camp. The camp's Jewish character was inherent in the pattern of its own values. It was symbolized by the effervescence of Jewish family life. Belsen forged a mighty ring of friendship among the survivors. Even after so many years, we are like one family. Although countries separate us, we are united by our suffering, our heritage, and by our determination that time not be permitted to obliterate the days of destruction of the Nazi period.

Before leaving Belsen, Yossel and I went again to the mass graves, said kaddish, and pledged that we would always carry the dead in our hearts. The AJDC gave each member of the Central Committee's Executive Committee the sum of $3,000 to enable us to take the first steps of our new life. When Yossel and I settled in the United States in 1958, we made a contribution to the United Jewish Appeal as an act of gratitude and repayment.

About 1,000 Jews, however, were still waiting for visas to emigrate. Many of them suffered from tuberculosis and other illnesses. Yossel went with them to a transit camp, Jever, near Bremen, where they remained until August 1, 1951, when they finally emigrated to various countries. I decided not to go to Jever. Since the day of liberation, I had been working in Belsen without interruption. I needed to be away from camps and needed a rest. In early September, Yossel took me and our two-year-old boy to Montreux, Switzerland, where our friends in the World Jewish Congress helped us rent two rooms in a family hotel. Yossel went back to Jever and remained there for a year, until the last Jew left. I visited from time to time, then joined him in Hamburg for the official ceremony marking the closing of the Jever camp, and with it the end of the chapter of the Jewish DPs in the British zone of Germany. Lord Henderson, the British Under Secretary of State for Foreign Affairs, was unable to attend but sent the following message:

> I should not wish the departure of the last Jewish Displaced Persons from the British Zone of Germany to take place without wishing them Godspeed. May the fine human qualities which have sustained them in the past years of adversity reap their reward in their new homeland.

We then returned to Montreux and started a new life. Our friends from London introduced Yossel to Swiss bankers and vouched for him, and he started a successful business in finance and real estate.

Six years later, Alex Easterman of the World Jewish Congress summed up the political significance of the Belsen DP camp and its leadership in the postwar years:

> Many a time and oft, my late colleague, Noah Barou, and I were awakened during the night by telephone calls from Josef Rosensaft. Now there was a problem of the refusal of the Central Committee to have armed non-Jewish guards. Then there was a dispute about enclosing the camp with barbed wire. Next, there was the resistance of the Committee against military search of homes and premises for alleged concealment of arms or the hoarding of illegal supplies. Again, there was conflict concerning assemblies of protest against Ernest Bevin's Palestine policies and actions. And a hundred more issues requiring negotiation, tact and patience, but always involving rights and resistance to infraction of liberties.
>
> Invariably, in the battles with Authority, the Central Committee won the day. Often, there was rancour and frustration on both sides. But, in the final analysis, the Jewish Displaced Persons of Belsen, and Rosensaft, their leader, won the respect of the British authorities who came to recognize that the motive force impelling what seemed to be defiance

and resistance was an indomitable spirit which the affliction of the Nazi horror camps had failed to quench and a matchless courage which suffering had vitalised. They came to understand, too, that the issues on which the Jewish Displaced Persons came in conflict with them, concerned no matters of trivial import, but related, fundamentally, to principles of political liberty and human justice. Bitter as the disputes often were, distaste and distrust gave way progressively to understanding and even to admiration of the Displaced Persons' implacable stand for their principles. They had shown toughness and grit, qualities which the British always understand and appreciate.

The deathless story of Belsen is not of the Jewish martyrs who lie in heaps in unvisited mass graves on the stark plains near the site of "Horror Camp No. 1," nor on the gaunt memorial obelisk which overlooks them. The Belsen story is the immortal epic for immemorial veneration of brave men and women who lived with death but survived to stand valiantly for freedom and right.[7]

With the closing of the Belsen DP camp, two problems remained. We rejected the British proposal that the care and maintenance of the Bergen-Belsen burial grounds be handed over to the German government and insisted that the mass graves come under international supervision. The World Jewish Congress in London supported us, and the matter was raised with the British Foreign Office, but we ultimately lost this fight.

Another problem was the creation of an international monument in Belsen. At the end of 1944, the Germans had captured two British soldiers, and instead of putting them into a POW camp, sent them to the Belsen concentration camp. Shortly before liberation, the Germans decided to get rid of troublesome witnesses and therefore took the British soldiers out of the barrack and shot them. One of the murdered soldiers was a nephew of the British Lt. General Sir Gordon Macready, who was briefly stationed with the British occupying administration in Hanover. As a gesture to his martyred nephew, the general came up with the idea of creating an international monument with an inscription in all 14 languages of those who

7. *Belsen, op. cit.,* pp. 92–93.

died in Belsen. Because 90 percent of the victims were Jews, we insisted on having both a Hebrew and a Yiddish inscription in the center. After long negotiations, we succeeded. The monument is a tall obelisk with a long wall. In the center an inscription reads, "To the memory of all those who died in this place."

The dedication ceremony for this monument was planned to take place in 1950, before the closing of the camp, but it was postponed on the demand of the Central Committee until the future care of the burial site could be decided upon. The unveiling ceremony took place in 1952 in the presence of representatives of the British government, British officers stationed near Belsen, Yossel, WJC president Nahum Goldmann, Dr. Barou, and Rabbi Isaac Levy, who came from London to deliver the invocation. The West German government was represented by its president, Theodor Heuss.

CHAPTER 13

Reparations from Germany

At the end of November 1945, when Shlomo Adler Rudel of the Jewish Agency for Palestine in London visited Belsen with an offer to take some of our Jewish orphans to Great Britain, he told us that during the war plans had already been made to call for indemnification of the Jewish people for the loss of their properties in Germany and all the countries occupied by Germany. Those plans, he said, had been prepared by Adler Rudel, Nehemiah and Jacob Robinson in the United States, and Siegfried Moses in Palestine. He also told us that in September 1945, Chaim Weizmann, on behalf of the Jewish Agency for Palestine, had presented the first official claim for restitution to the four big powers—the United States, France, Great Britain, and the Soviet Union. We listened politely but did not express interest. At that time, all our efforts and thoughts were on how to organize ourselves in Belsen to live a decent, human, social and cultural life during our temporary stay there.

In 1949, West Germany became an independent state under Chancellor Konrad Adenauer, who had been an opponent of the Nazis. As there were no formal relations between Israel and West Germany, the Israel government in early 1951 sent a note to the four powers demanding reparations on behalf of the Jewish people in the amount of $1.5 billion. The reply from the United States, France, and Great Britain was that Israel had to negotiate any such restitution directly with the West German government.

In the meantime, Noah Barou had also become involved in discussions regarding

German reparations. A German Jew named Gerhard Lewy, who had left Germany for London during the 1930s, had contacted Barou in London and told him that Lewy had been a classmate of Herbert Blankenhorn, then political director of the West German Foreign Ministry and one of Adenauer's closest advisors. Lewy offered to use his influence with Blankenhorn in connection with the restitution of heirless Jewish properties. On July 14, 1951, Barou wrote to Yossel in Jever, asking him to go to Bonn to meet with Lewy, which Yossel did. After that meeting, Yossel and Barou met with Nahum Goldmann and suggested that he, in his capacity as president of the World Jewish Congress, undertake negotiations with West Germany on behalf of the Jewish people.

Lengthy and complicated meetings and discussions followed throughout 1951 and 1952, culminating in the Reparations Agreements executed by the State of Israel, West Germany, and Goldmann on behalf of the Conference on Jewish Material Claims Against Germany, a body created in October 1951 to represent Diaspora Jewry in the negotiations. Goldmann and Barou asked Yossel to help behind the scenes. Yossel then met with Blankenhorn, and they devised a plan of action. Yossel also met with Ludwig Erhard, the West German economics minister, and Walter Hallstein, secretary of state of the Ministry of Foreign Affairs and the de facto West German foreign minister. Yossel made countless trips to Bonn, Cologne, and London, as well as thousands of telephone calls. He sent many cables and letters, and forwarded messages, but he never accepted any reimbursement. His friend Jack Birnbaum, who lived in Cologne, gave Yossel a place to stay. With Blankenhorn's help, Yossel arranged numerous secret meetings between Barou, Goldmann, and members of the German government who were involved in the negotiations. They made up a code to be used in letters and cables instead of names. Adenauer was the *"Zaken"* (Hebrew for "old one"), Blankenhorn was "Bruno," Hallstein was "Harry," Erhard was "Leo," and Fritz Schäffer, the West German Finance Minister, was *"Kalkala"* (Hebrew for finance).

The full story of Yossel's involvement in these negotiations remains to be told. On October 12, 1952, after the Luxembourg Agreements had been signed, Goldmann wrote to Yossel as follows:

> Dear Friend,
> Now that the agreement with Germany has been signed, I would like

to express my personal thanks and deep appreciation for your cooperation in those difficult months as well as the thanks and appreciation of the Jewish Agency and Claims Conference. What you have accomplished was of the greatest significance for the successful development of the negotiations. You had to undertake many difficult missions and you did it with great tact and understanding. I do not even mention your personal hardship during the many trips I asked you to make. Your cooperation was of invaluable importance for me personally. The fact that your work was behind the scenes heightens its value and urges me to express my deepest recognition. That the negotiations ended in relatively short time and very successfully will be, as I know you, the best reward for your laborious efforts.

Yossel's long absences made a powerful impression on our son. We never realized how much Meni missed his father until one day a friend of ours asked what he would like to be when he grew up. Meni answered, "A barber." Our friend asked him why. Meni answered, "Because whenever Claude [his kindergarten friend] comes home, his father [a barber] is always there."

Following the signing of the Reparations Agreement, a purchasing mission from Israel, headed by Felix Shinnar, representing the Israeli Ministry of Commerce and Industry, was established in Cologne. Yossel helped them whenever he was asked. Many German firms were involved. Some wanted to do business with Yossel, but he refused to do any business with the Germans or in Germany.

Initially, Yossel and I decided that neither of us would accept individual reparations from Germany. We felt that no amount of money could compensate for our loss, and we did not want to appear to be accepting it as such. But then a delegation of survivors came to see Yossel and made the practical point that if we didn't accept reparations, other Holocaust survivors, especially those from Belsen, might not do so either. And some of the people foregoing reparations would really need the money. So we accepted the minimum amount—not as payment for our suffering or to cancel Germany's debt to the Jewish people, but in the sense that the Germans should pay back at least a part of what they had stolen from us. I believe it is important to remember that reparation is a legal issue, not a moral one; the payment of money can never be viewed as the payment of a moral debt.

CHAPTER 14

A New Life

L ife in Montreux was very quiet. We had no friends except those who visited occasionally from the United States or Israel. To interrupt the boredom, I used to go by overnight train to Paris, spend a day there, and return refreshed. Yossel's business activities and Jewish political events kept him busy. In the early summer of 1952, we took our first real vacation. I was suffering from liver and gall-bladder infections caused by the untreated malaria I had in Birkenau, so we went to Vulpera, a spa in the Swiss mountains. That August, we rented a car with a driver and explored parts of Switzerland and Italy. After a brief but disastrous visit to Viareggio, where Meni was severely bitten by mosquitoes, we drove along the Mediterranean coast to San Remo, on the Italian Riviera. There we discovered the magnificent Royal Hotel, with its enormous swimming pool and beautiful grounds. We stayed for two weeks, then returned every year thereafter. It became our summer home, the one place where I can truly relax.

In October 1952, we went to New York, where we met many of our Belsen friends, as well as Yossel's first cousin Hela Saender, her husband Chaskel, and their daughter Susan. We then went to Chicago to visit the Weintraubs and Silberniks, our friends and next-door neighbors from *Kantine* 2 in Belsen.

After our return to Montreux, Meni started kindergarten in a French-language school. One of his classmates was Josephine Chaplin, the second daughter of Charlie Chaplin, to whose estate in nearby Vevey Meni was often invited on weekends. Thanks to the children's friendship, we met Charlie Chaplin, his wife, Oona, and their other children. On our first visit to their home for a Friday night dinner, there were only the immediate family members and Chaplin's brother, Sidney. After dinner, after the children had gone to play, Charlie Chaplin asked us about the camps and Belsen. We told him about our experiences and mentioned that we had just returned from Belsen, where we had paid our respects to the dead buried in its mass graves. Sidney Chaplin was surprised and asked why we tortured ourselves so; why we did not try to erase those tragic experiences from our memory. Before we had the chance to reply, Charlie Chaplin said that he understood us very well. He told us that his family was very poor. One day when he was a young boy, his mother got sick. He carried her in his arms to the hospital as he did not have any money for transportation. Years later, after he had become famous and rich, he never forgot his poor youth and his mother. Whenever he was in London, before going to his hotel, his first visit was to the place where he was born. He would stand for a while on the street, looking up at the window where his mother used to stand.

Like all Swiss schools, Meni's had a long December–January holiday in addition to the summer vacation. Because Meni wanted very much to learn to ski, we took him to Arosa in the Swiss Alps. He became an excellent skier, much to Yossel's and my delight. Arosa was like an enchanted world, a small mountain place, not yet spoiled by progress. Cars were not allowed to stay around the hotels but had to be left near the railroad station. I used to get up early in the morning and go out for a walk before anyone else was awake. It used to snow in Poland, but this was different. The snow in Arosa was white, untouched. Above was the blue sky and a silence that you could almost touch. I never felt so close to God as in those moments.

As I have already mentioned, in the early 1950s Israel's economic situation was very difficult, with food rationing and other austerity programs. Yossel and I tried to help as much as we could. We sent hundreds of food packages to our *Belsener* friends and others in Israel, many of whom we never met. One day, we received a letter from a desperate father who wrote that although he had never met Yossel, he had heard about his good heart and deeds. He had a 12-year-old daughter who would lose her eyesight unless she had surgery, and the only doctor who could cure her was a certain Dr. Franconi in Switzerland. Yossel immediately got in touch with Joseph Linton, Chaim Weizmann's former private secretary who was then Israel's Ambassador in Bern. Yossel asked the Ambassador to arrange passage to Switzerland for the girl on El Al, and promised that we would take care of all medical and hospital expenses. This was done, and after many months, the girl returned to Israel cured.

We did not realize that Meni was listening to our conversations. One day he came to me saying that he too would like to do something to help the less fortunate as he knew that charity, *tzedakah,* is an important part of our Jewish tradition. I was touched by this and came up with an idea. In Trogen, Switzerland, there is a home for abandoned children as well as those from broken marriages and asocial parents, called the Pestalozzi Village, after the well-known educator. I suggested to Meni that from time to time he choose some of his toys and send them to the children, which he did.

We often thought of the Belsen survivors who had been taken to Sweden shortly after the liberation by Count Folke Bernadotte and the Swedish Red Cross. When we visited Stockholm in 1955, one of them told us: "Life in Sweden is quiet. Here a child does not cry, a rooster does not crow, a tramway does not ring, and people do not talk. We live a quiet life." We also learned that some of the critically ill survivors had died in 1945 in the city of Malmö and were buried in the Jewish cemetery there, next to the wall, like outcasts. Yossel expressed his outrage to the leaders of the Swedish Jewish community and made sure that these dead at last received a decent burial.

In 1956, we took Meni to Israel for the first time, to celebrate his eighth birthday. There he met our friends and other children who had also been born in the Belsen DP camp. He developed friendships with some that have lasted until today. He also met a group of 25 of my former "children," the orphans from Belsen, who brought their children, and I overheard him saying to one of his friends, "Did you see how many grandchildren my mother has?"

We spent most of our time in Israel at the seaside Sharon Hotel in Herzlia, near Tel Aviv, but also went to Jerusalem for several days, to see old friends and to show off Meni. Understandably, he was bored, especially since he spoke neither English nor Hebrew at the time. We were still living in Montreux, and he spoke French and German. One Saturday afternoon we were invited to the residence of Moshe Sharett, then the minister of foreign affairs, along with members of the government and diplomats. The discussions did not interest Meni, who wandered around the house looking at mementos that Sharett had received in different countries. Sharett noticed that Meni was all alone, walked over to him, and sat down and spoke with him in

French for a good half hour, explaining about the origins of the various items in the room and asking him how he liked Israel and what he liked to study. They promised to write to each other and developed a friendship that lasted until the last months of Sharett's life.

In 1958 a serious problem arose concerning the mass graves in Belsen. The French Mission for the Search of Victims of War wanted to exhume, identify, and return to France the 139 French nationals who had died in Belsen and were buried with thousands of others in the mass graves. Yossel opposed any such exhumation in the name of the survivors of Belsen on two grounds. First, in 1945 it was almost impossible to tell a dead man from a woman. So many bodies had been bulldozed into the mass graves. Did they think that 13 years later they would be able to tell French bones from the others? The idea was macabre. And second, we believed that to disturb the remains of the victims would be an act of desecration.

Many people joined us in our fight: scientists, lawyers, rabbis. The dispute, which lasted more than 11 years, was eventually brought before an arbitration commission composed of two Swedish judges, one Swiss, three Germans, one French, one British, and one American. Yossel suggested that the nine members of the commission go to Belsen to see the mass graves for themselves, and on May 6, 1969, accompanied by Yossel, they did so and were shocked by what they saw. One of the commission members expressed surprise that Yossel had made a special trip to Belsen from New York. Yossel answered, "How could I not come?" Before leaving Belsen, one of the judges said, "Indeed the case is macabre and so is our visit."

Largely as the result of Yossel's untiring efforts, the dispute was finally resolved in our favor. On October 30, 1969, the commission met in Koblenz and issued its decision against the exhumation. Meni wrote his M.A. thesis in modern western European history at Columbia University about this controversy.[8] In the "Conclusion," he wrote:

> In the final analysis, the confrontation over the Bergen-Belsen mass graves must be seen as a moral struggle, and its outcome as a moral victory. It was one of the rare instances in history in which political

---

8. Menachem Z. Rosensaft, "The Mass Graves of Bergen-Belsen: Focus for Confrontation," *Jewish Social Studies*, vol. xli, no. 2 (1979).

expedience, governmental power and amoral pragmatism gave way before ethical and human considerations. The very fact that the dispute was allowed to occur was an indictment against the French Government which precipitated it; and the decision of the arbitration commission vindicated those who believed that at least in death the victims of the Holocaust deserved to be left to rest in dignity.

In August 1959, during the third plenary session of the World Jewish Congress in Stockholm, it was decided to build a museum to the Jewish Diaspora in Israel. A special committee was appointed to implement the assembly's decision and determine the form of this project. Yossel was asked by Nahum Goldmann to serve on this committee, and we immediately made our contribution. Yossel bought a piece of land in Tel Aviv and donated it for this project. Later, Tel Aviv University expressed its wish to have the museum on its grounds. The land was then sold, and the proceeds were used to build Beit Hatefutsoth, the Nahum Goldmann Museum of the Jewish Diaspora, which became one of Israel's most important cultural institutions.

CHAPTER 15

Coming to New York

In 1958, we left Montreux for New York. We enrolled Meni in the Ethical Culture School on Manhattan's West Side, and he then went on to that school's high school, the Fieldston School, from which he graduated in 1966. Many of our friends were surprised that we did not send him to a Jewish school, but I had my reasons. The Ethical Culture School was attended by children of different religions, different cultures, and different races. I wanted Meni to be exposed to the real world. That is why I thought this school was the right choice.

For almost two years, we lived at the Alden Hotel on Central Park West. One day the telephone rang. I answered the phone and almost screamed. It was Lonia, my friend from Birkenau. She had found out where I was—I didn't even know that she had survived. We met the same evening; it turned out that she lived around the corner from the Alden. We laughed and cried when we saw each other. I was delighted to learn that Lonia had experienced one of those miracles: she was reunited with her husband, who had also survived life in a camp, and with their son, who had been hidden by Polish Christians throughout the war.[9]

In the spring of 1960, we moved to our own apartment at 30 East 71st Street. It was the first real home for Yossel and me since the ghettos in Poland. We opened our home symbolically on April 15, the anniversary of our liberation at Belsen, and

---

9. Lonia's husband was Alexander Donat, author of *The Holocaust Kingdom* (Washington, D.C.: United States Holocaust Memorial Museum, 1999).

invited our Belsen friends to celebrate with us. Thereafter, we got together every year on that date.

After we settled in New York, I wanted to get my American diploma in order to start a private practice, but I postponed this plan for several reasons. We had just come to a new country; Meni had just started a new school, he didn't know English, and he had not yet made new friends. Also, Yossel was traveling a lot on business. I hated to think that when Meni came home from school, neither of his parents would be there. So I decided to make our home my priority and never went back to the university. I often missed my profession, but I never regretted my decision.

Our home was always open to our and to Meni's friends as well as to many prominent Jewish personalities, including Israeli political leaders and American Jewish intellectuals. A frequent visitor was the author Elie Wiesel, a child survivor of Auschwitz and Buchenwald. He immediately found a common language with Yossel. They could sit for hours, conversing in Yiddish. They both had beautiful voices, and we loved to listen to them sing Yiddish folk songs and Hasidic melodies.

Another friend who used to come often was Mannes Schwarz, whom we knew from Belsen. After the Jever DP camp was closed, he stayed in Germany for a while. In 1951, he had a terrible car accident there. When we heard the news, Yossel immediately flew to Hamburg to see Mannes in the hospital. It was several years until he was physically able to come to New York to join his brother and sister. He became a successful business executive, representing one of the major Swiss watch companies in the United States. Together with Norbert Wollheim, Sam Bloch, Yossel, and me, Mannes was one of the leaders of our Belsen survivors' group in New York. One day, when Mannes came to see us, he met a young woman, Malka Silberberg, who had survived the war in Siberia together with her parents, lived in the Belsen DP camp for some years, and then settled in Israel where she served in the army. She had a tremendous voice and had won a scholarship to study at the Juilliard School of Music in New York. She and Mannes fell in love and married in our home on March 14, 1965. They live in New York, have two lovely daughters, Ghitta and Tirza, and are among my very dearest friends.

We made new friends in New York as well, among them Joseph and Sonia Breindel. Joseph is a Polish Jew who studied medicine in Italy before the war and became a prominent gynecologist in New York. Sonia, born in Luxembourg, survived the war with her mother, first in France and then, from 1942 until 1945, in an intern-ment camp in Switzerland. Her father was killed in Auschwitz. Their son, Eric, who was often in our home as a child, became a columnist and the editorial page editor of the *New York Post*. He writes frequently about the Holocaust in the context of contemporary events, and I like to think that his views were influenced to some extent by his exposure to Yossel while he was growing up.

Our home was also a place of rest for some of the Israeli dignitaries who happened to be our friends. One of them, Pinchas Sapir, Israel's minister of commerce and industry and later finance minister, used to say that our home was the only place outside his own where he could rest. He used to come to us after a busy day, take off his shoes, rest on the sofa, and sip a cup of tea. Nobody disturbed him.

Meni's friends were also always in our home as he was growing up. His closest friends were Robert Fagenson, Sandra Gabrilove, and Jeffrey Katz. They have kept their friendship over the years, and I have watched them mature into delightful, successful adults. They became my young friends as well.

On June 17, 1961, we celebrated Meni's Bar Mitzvah in Israel at the Sharon Hotel in Herzlia, surrounded by our Belsen friends from Israel and abroad. Meni read his haftarah beautifully. As I listened to and looked at him, I visualized members of my family sitting with us. We asked Meni what Bar Mitzvah present he would like from us, and without hesitation he said, "I would like to go to Belsen to see the place where I was born." We were touched and we took him there for the first time since he had left as a two-year-old. He saw the mass graves, the Jewish Monu-ment, and the International Monument. We took him to the hospital where he was born. He did not utter a word. It was not until years later that he expressed his feel-ings in his poems, articles, and lectures.

On January 29, 1962, I became an American citizen. When my first American passport was in my hand, I was thinking how many identities I had already had in my life. Having been born in Poland, I was a Polish citizen. In my Polish passport was my identity: Jewish. Then came the war, and I got a German ID card, and Sarah was added to my name. When we went to the ghetto, I had another ID. After the big selection in August 1942, I got a new card, the *Sonderkarte*. It meant that I was "safe" and able to work. Then I was deported to Auschwitz-Birkenau where I re-ceived a mark of distinction. I still have it, the blue number tattooed on my left arm: 52406, with a triangle underneath, signifying that I was Jewish and had become a number only. Then I was sent to Belsen, where I was known by another number: 10260. After liberation, I was a displaced person with a DP card. Then we went to Switzerland, where I held a stateless passport. I then immigrated to the United States and received a green card. Finally, as I was holding an American passport, a strange feeling overcame me. It was a feeling of belonging.

Yossel loved paintings. He had seen and experienced so much ugliness that he now wanted to be surrounded by beautiful things; so he became an art collector. He had a wonderful eye and great intuition. In time, our collection included works by Renoir, Monet, Pissarro, Sisley, Picasso, Braque, Gris, Chagall, and other impressionists and post-impressionists. We had the opportunity to meet Marc Chagall. He and his wife, Vava, visited us several times in New York, and I treated them to Russian borscht. Interestingly, Chagall, from Vitebsk, and Yossel, from Będzin, immediately found a common language. During the many visits that followed our first meeting, they sat for hours, speaking Yiddish and reminiscing about their youth.

In early June 1967, we were about to leave for Israel when news came that Israel had been attacked by Arab countries and that war had started. We prayed that Israel would not be harmed. We were in touch with many of our friends whose children were on the battlefield, but a miracle happened. The war lasted only six days, and Israel was victorious. As a result, the Israeli army occupied the Gaza Strip, the West Bank, and East Jerusalem.

Soon after the end of the war, the three of us went to Israel. The airport was dark, without lights. Our friends were waiting for us. They were still shaking and scared, not able to believe that the war was over, and still worrying about their children. But they were happy to see us. We visited numerous Israeli political leaders, including Ben-Gurion and Teddy Kollek, the mayor of Jerusalem. Ben-Gurion said that now Israel should return all the Arab territories it had occupied except Jerusalem. He did not want Israel to become a nation of occupation. In addition, he could foresee a lot of trouble in the future from the local Arab population if Israel did not return this land. Most of the people in the room were shocked, but subsequent events have proved that Ben-Gurion was right.

Meni wanted to see Gaza, so one day I went with him. (Yossel was in Europe.) It was a rather foolish thing to do. As we were approaching Gaza, I noticed that our driver had put a loaded revolver on the seat next to him. He also warned us not to open a window, even if we saw begging children. A few days later Yossel,

Meni, and I went to a military hospital near Tel Aviv where our friend Dr. Chaim Sheba led us past men who had been severely wounded in the skirmishes. We saw soldiers who had lost their legs and arms, soldiers who had lost their sight and were blind—all invalids for life. After having seen this suffering, Yossel and I decided to do something to help the families of the fallen soldiers and the invalids. In addition to making a monetary contribution to the hospital, we decided to publish the *Book of Heroism (Sefer ha-Gevurah),* with the consent and help of the Israeli army and the Organization of Journalists in Tel Aviv. The contents included accounts of the first hours of the Six-Day War, articles by the generals and commanding officers, and stories about the fallen officers and enlisted soldiers. The Israel Ministry of Defense established a fund for the families of the fallen soldiers and to provide scholarships for their children.

In 1970, we observed the 25th anniversary of our liberation by making a pilgrimage to Belsen. We were joined on that occasion by Elie and Marion Wiesel, our liberator Brigadier General Glyn Hughes, and many *Belseners.* When we arrived there, it was raining. Subsequently, the Jewish philosopher Emil Fackenheim wrote that Yossel had observed: "We have revisited this place of our suffering many times. It always rains. God weeps. He weeps for the sins he has committed against his people Israel."[10] Later that summer, Elie and Marion Wiesel were our guests in San Remo. On August 26, 1970, my birthday, Yossel wrote a letter from San Remo to the Nobel Committee in Oslo on behalf of the World Federation of Bergen-Belsen Associations supporting Elie's nomination for the Nobel Peace Prize, which he subsequently received in 1986. If I am not mistaken, this letter was one of the first to support Elie's candidacy. Two years later, when Elie and Marion's son, Elisha, was born, I was asked to be his godmother.

Meni received his B.A. and M.A. degrees with honors from The Johns Hopkins University and returned to New York to continue his studies at Columbia University, where he earned a second M.A. in modern western European history. At the same time, he was lecturing about the Holocaust at the City College of New York, assisting Elie Wiesel.

One of our happiest days was January 13, 1974, when Meni married Jeanie Bloch, the daughter of our dear friends Lilly and Sam Bloch, whom we had met in Belsen

---

10. Emil L. Fackenheim, *The Jewish Return into History* (New York: Schocken Publishers, 1978), p. 125.

soon after the war. At the outbreak of the German-Soviet war in 1941, Lilly, who was then 12 years old, and her parents, Rose and David Czaban, were in Podwoloczyska, near Ternopol, in eastern Galicia. The city was captured by the Germans, but thanks to a Christian family who gave them a place to hide, Lilly, an only child, her parents, and her mother's sister all survived. The Czabans came to the Belsen DP camp in early 1946, and Lilly studied dentistry at the University of Bonn.

Sam Bloch, the son of Jehoshua and Sonia Bloch, was born and lived in Ivye, a small town in northeast Poland, now Belarus. His father, an ardent Zionist, spoke only Hebrew to Sam and sent him to study in Vilna (present-day Vilnius). When the war started, Sam returned home to be with his parents and baby brother. Ivye first was occupied by the Russians, then on July 1, 1941, it was captured by the Germans. Many members of the town's Jewish intelligentsia, among them Sam's father, were murdered on Tishah b'Av, the Jewish fast day commemorating the destruction of the Temple in Jerusalem. Sam went into the forest and joined the partisan group headed by Tuvia Bielski. Sam was able to save his mother and brother, and they came to Belsen at the end of 1945. Sam represented the Zionist party, Ha-Shomer ha-Tsa'ir, on the Belsen Jewish Committee. He and Lilly met in Belsen and they were married in 1949. At their wedding, Yossel and I brought Sam to the *hupah*, the wedding canopy, because his widowed mother did not want to do so on her own.

Sam and Lilly then immigrated to the United States. They have two daughters, Jeanie and Gloria. Jeanie, the elder, is beautiful, extremely intelligent, and, as an alumna of Barnard College, very well educated. A brilliant art historian, she has written and published outstanding articles on Camille Pissarro and other artists. A former curator and assistant director of education at New York's Jewish Museum, she is now the National Director for Public Affairs and Institutional Planning at Hebrew Union College-Jewish Institute of Religion in New York. I have a wonderful relationship with her and love and respect her. She has become not just *like* a daughter to me, but she has become, and *is*, my daughter in every sense of the word. No daughter could be more caring, more loving, more wonderful than Jeanie has been to me.

Sam worked closely with Yossel in creating our Bergen-Belsen survivors' group in New York and organizing all its activities. While Yossel was alive, Sam was the Secretary General of the World Federation of Bergen-Belsen Associations, and he is now its president. He is also the senior vice president of the American Gathering of Jewish Holocaust Survivors and chairman of the board of the American Friends of Beit Hatefutsoth. Lilly and Sam are more than my family; they are my closest and dearest friends.

When Jeanie and Meni were married, both sets of parents led them to the *hupah*. Jeanie's sister, Gloria, was the maid of honor, and Robert Fagenson was Meni's best man. The ceremony, which took place in our home, was performed by two rabbis, both good friends of ours: Dr. Gerson D. Cohen, a Conservative rabbi and Chancellor of the Jewish Theological Seminary of America, and Rabbi Joseph Lookstein, an Orthodox rabbi who was President of Bar Ilan University in Israel. Elie Wiesel also participated in the ceremony. The *ketubah* was a Conservative one brought by Rabbi Cohen, and Rabbi Lookstein signed it as a witness. Jeanie's wedding ring was the ring my father had originally made for me. Lilly and Sam then hosted a beautiful wedding party, a real Jewish *simha,* which was attended by many of our friends.

CHAPTER 16

Belsen Survivors after 1950

After they settled in different countries, the survivors of Belsen did not stop their activities: they started to organize. We were the first, and for many years the only, organization of survivors founded with the aim of telling the world what had happened to the Jewish people during the Holocaust and keeping the memory of our martyrs alive. In 1951, an organization of Belsen survivors, the Irgun Sherit ha-Pletah, was established in Israel under the leadership of Raphael Olewski, Hela and Jacob Berlinski, Zvi Azaria, Chaim Posluszny, Romek Zynger, and Efraim Londner. In 1959, Belsen organizations were established in Toronto, chaired by Berl Laufer, and in Montreal, chaired by Paul Trepman. We established the Bergen-Belsen Association in New York, whose leadership included, in addition to Yossel and myself, Norbert Wollheim, Sam Bloch, Mannes Schwarz, David Rosenthal, Mendel Butnick, Jack Rosmarin, Israel Krakowski, Isidore Guterman, Joseph Rosenberg, and Abrasha Funk. There was also a group of Belsen survivors in Chicago, headed by Samuel Weintraub and Max Silbernik. In 1963, we created the World Federation of Bergen-Belsen Associations, made up of the various Belsen groups throughout the world, with Yossel as president, Norbert Wollheim as vice-president, and Sam Bloch as secretary-general. Our aim was to maintain contact among people who shared memories of common suffering and to extend help where needed.

In Israel, we established an interest-free scholarship and loan fund, which I chaired. We met annually in Israel and New York and often made pilgrimages to the mass graves of Belsen. Each time, we said kaddish, remembered, and renewed our oath that we would never forget. Each time, we renewed our pledge that we were leaving our legacy to our children and the generations to come so that they would know what the Germans had done to the Jewish people. To mark the tenth anniversary of our liberation, a forest, Ya'ar Belsen, was planted in the Judean Hills, near Jerusalem. For that moving ceremony, on Sunday, April 24, 1955, our liberator Brigadier General Glyn Hughes and his wife came especially from London. On Mount Zion in Jerusalem, near the entrance to the Cave of the Holocaust, we erected a monument modeled on the one that stands in Belsen.

We published two books that tell the story of Belsen before and especially after the liberation: *Belsen,* published in 1957, and *Holocaust and Rebirth,* edited by Sam Bloch, published in 1965. In 1963, we brought Gideon Hausner to New York for his first American public appearance after the Eichmann Trial, and we published a monograph by the Israeli writer K. Shabbetai, *As Sheep to the Slaughter?,* refuting the myth that European Jews had passively allowed themselves to be murdered by the Germans without resisting. We also published books dealing with the Holocaust in English, Hebrew, and Yiddish, including a special edition of Elie Wiesel's *The Town Beyond the Wall;* two volumes of poetry by Aaron Zeitlin; *Than a Tear in the Sea* by Mannes Sperber; *The Forest My Friend* by Donia Rosen; *The Seven Little Lanes* by Chaim Grade; and *I Do Remind,* a volume of Yiddish poems by Jacob Glatstein.

As we approached the 20th anniversary of our liberation, Meni and some of the other children born in Belsen, by then all teenagers, decided to record their perspective on the Holocaust and their identity as children of survivors. In 1965, we published the *Bergen-Belsen Youth Magazine,* edited by Meni, consisting of articles, poems, and short stories by our children. To the best of my knowledge, it was the first organized effort anywhere by sons and daughters of Holocaust survivors. That year, we also issued a record of songs of the Holocaust sung by the Yiddish singer Sidor Belarsky.

Also in 1965, in order to raise awareness of the Holocaust, we established the International Remembrance Award for outstanding books on the Holocaust, with the following purpose:

> The World Federation of Bergen-Belsen Associations established the
> Remembrance Award for excellence and distinction in literature with
> the objective of giving recognition to literary works which derive their

inspiration from the Holocaust experience, and encouraging creativity and research into the history of Jewish martyrdom and resistance.

The ideas and hopes which are embodied in the Remembrance Award are a further expression of our determination to perpetuate the memory of Jewish suffering and heroism till the end of time.

Elie Wiesel was the first recipient of our Remembrance Award and thereafter chaired its international jury, which included Professors Emil Fackenheim and George Steiner; the Dutch Jewish historian Jacob Presser; Israeli journalist David Lazar; the Yiddish literary critic Shlomo Bickel; the novelist Piotr Rawicz, himself a survivor; and the great Yiddish poet Jacob Glatstein. Our organization was represented by Sam Bloch, Norbert Wollheim, and myself, with Yossel serving ex officio. Other recipients of the award included the novelist Mannes Sperber; Arthur Morse, author of *While Six Million Died;* two great Yiddish authors, both Holocaust survivors, Avraham Sutzkever and Chaim Grade; and the Israeli Hebrew-language poets Abba Kovner and Uri Tzvi Greenberg.

As part of the 20th anniversary of our liberation, we also wanted to express our gratitude to our British liberators. As we had just published the book *Holocaust and Rebirth,* we decided to give a dinner at the Savoy Hotel in London to both mark the publication of this commemorative album and pay tribute to the British army. Our guest speaker was the wartime British foreign minister, Sir Anthony Eden. Among the guests were Brigadier General Glyn Hughes; Brigadier General James Johnston; Captain Derrick Sington, the first British officer to enter Belsen on April 15, 1945, and announce the liberation of the camp; Major General Sir Evelyn D. Fenshaw; the actor Leo Genn, who had been a member of the prosecution team at the Belsen trial; Sir Barnet Janner, M.P., president of the British Board of Deputies; and the Israeli Ambassador Aaron Remez. Meni was there with his friend Jeff Katz, and we took great pride in introducing our son to our liberators. It was a beautiful, meaningful evening.

The following day I was invited for tea at the home of Brigadier General Glyn Hughes and his wife. When I opened the door, I saw many of the British doctors and nurses with whom I had worked in Belsen right after the liberation. I was moved by this surprise and grateful for this gesture. We sat for hours recollecting our memories and the experiences of our collaboration.

We used to have annual dinners at the Sharon Hotel in Herzlia, Israel, to celebrate the anniversary of our liberation. In addition to our fellow Belsen survivors, many prominent personalities in Israeli political, cultural, and economic life attended, including Moshe Sharett, Levi Eshkol, Golda Meir, and Abba Eban. At one of these evenings, Sharett made a toast in which he expressed his amazement that the survivors of Belsen had started and maintained this annual tradition. Yossel responded, "Since neither the Israel government nor anyone else took the initiative to celebrate our survival, we had to do it ourselves."

At another Belsen evening in the early 1960s, we had an unexpected guest— Marlene Dietrich, on her first tour in Israel. Before the war, her daughter had been a classmate of the daughter of Harry and Rose Levi, who managed the Sharon Hotel. The young Miss Levi had died of cancer two years earlier, and Miss Dietrich had come to visit the Levis after going to their daughter's grave. When she heard about our dinner, Miss Dietrich asked if she could come. She was welcomed very warmly. When she noticed the blue tattooed number on the arm of a woman survivor, she kissed the spot. We knew that Miss Dietrich, a German, was an anti-Nazi and had helped her Jewish friends get out of Germany.

In 1975, on the 30th anniversary of our liberation, we had a get-together of *Belseners* and other friends of Belsen in New York City, after which we went to Israel and gave a dinner at the King David Hotel in Jerusalem. It was to be Yossel's last public appearance. Prime Minister Yitzhak Rabin was our guest speaker. As it happened, the dinner took place the evening before Rabin's departure to Germany, the first such trip by an Israeli prime minister. While there, he was going to visit the Belsen mass graves. In his speech, Yossel addressed Rabin and said, "When you walk along the grass-covered graves, close your eyes and try to imagine us there, 30 years ago."

CHAPTER 17

Yossel's Death

It was just after Rosh Hashanah 1975. We had spent a beautiful vacation together in Israel, San Remo, and London. Meni and Jeanie had gone home to New York, and Yossel and I had remained in London for a few more days, over the Jewish New Year. On September 9, I returned to New York, and Yossel was supposed to follow two or three days later. The next morning, September 10, he called from London; everything was fine, and he was about to make his reservations to come home. A few hours later, Jeanie and Meni came to our apartment, pale, their eyes red. A friend of ours, Pinky Taylor, had called from London to tell Meni that Yossel had collapsed in the lobby of Claridge's Hotel. He was gone. I couldn't believe it. I had just spoken to him, and there had been no indication that anything was wrong, that he didn't feel well.

That evening, Meni, Jeanie, Sam, and I flew to London to bring Yossel back to New York. I was numb. I could not speak. I could not face the truth. The funeral was on Sunday, September 14, on the eve of Yom Kippur. I was told that the synagogue, Kehilath Jeshurun, was packed with people, but I did not see them. Yossel was eulogized by Rabbi Joseph Lookstein and Elie Wiesel, but I didn't hear a word they said. Then we went to the cemetery, and when Meni said kaddish, I broke down. We didn't sit shivah for the usual seven days of mourning because of Yom Kippur, which cut off the mourning period. The Day of Atonement services were held in our living room, with Elie Wiesel chanting the same prayers that Yossel had sung in Auschwitz 31 years before.

Our closest *Belsener* friends from Israel, Canada, and various parts of the United States came to the funeral and joined in the prayers. I did not attend the services; I felt that I could not take this shock, either mentally or physically. My body reacted: less than a week later, my gall bladder burst, and I was rushed to New York University Hospital, unconscious, with a fever of 106 degrees Fahrenheit. The situation was critical. My doctor, Abraham Sunshine, a brilliant and caring physician, got in touch with a great surgeon, Dr. Localio, who was flown in from his home in Connecticut by helicopter, and he saved me. (In later years, Dr. Sunshine, his partner Dr. Ted Listokin, and a liver specialist, Dr. Jonathan Cohen, continued to take wonderful care of me as the liver problems I had contracted in Auschwitz intensified.) The operation took many hours. The doctors allowed my dear friend Dr. Joseph Breindel to be in the operating room. I then was in intensive care for many days, fighting for my life. I was told that my children and Sam and Lilly were at the hospital all the time, and that other friends, especially Mannes and Malka Schwarz, were also there. I did not see anybody, or, if I did, I did not know it.

When I was well enough to return home, my children stayed with me for almost nine months. I admired Meni's strength and Jeanie's love and devotion. Lilly and Sam were wonderful. My other dear friends were also nearby. I found piles of mail— 898 letters of condolence and obituary notices from friends, presidents, diplomats, and so many others. I did not have the strength or courage to read them and was grateful to Meni and Jeanie when they told me that they had answered them all. It was ten years before I was ready to read those messages.

Our life became very different. Before our tragedy Meni had been planning to become a lawyer, but now he had to postpone his plans for a while. He took a great burden off my shoulders. How he found the strength, I never knew. Thirty days after Yossel's death, a special memorial and tribute to him took place in Israel, organized by the Israeli branch of the World Federation of Bergen-Belsen Associations. Meni went to attend this memorial service. Among the speakers were Nahum Goldmann and Gideon Hausner. Later, when I read Dr. Hausner's eulogy, one paragraph in particular struck me. He had captured an essential quality of Yossel that most people, even those who thought they knew him well, had missed:

> Yossel was a friendly person, a good-hearted person. He loved to meet
> with friends and talk till late at night. His words were filled with Jewish

wisdom and with humor. But upon disclosing his thoughts and his spiritual world, suddenly one could see his eyelids being lowered over his clear blue eyes as though he was overwhelmed by some inner mystery. It did not last long, and he resumed his talk and a smile again appeared on his face. It was then that one could sense that deep in his heart some mystery remained hidden, a mystery that could not find its verbal expression, but watched over him. Did the image of Auschwitz and Bergen-Belsen appear before his eyes at such moments?

One year after Yossel's death, we put up a monument above his grave, and Meni eulogized his father with the following poem:

> *Father*
> I used to be a part of you
> belong to you
> the extension of your being
> but now
> you live within me
> are the spark
> of my consciousness
>
> I say Kaddish for you
> > with you
> > as you
> sing your melodies
> speak your words
> hearing your voice in mine
> and my eyes
> too green
> have somehow started to reflect
> the blue of yours
>
> I used to be a part of you
> protected by your presence
> by your light

but now
the time is mine
and alone
I must be more than myself:
your son
has become your heir
has become you

We also received many telegrams and letters on this occasion, including a moving letter sent to Meni from the President of Israel, Ephraim Katzir:

> With the passing of the months since the loss of your remarkable fa-ther—the loss which is not only your family's but all Israel's—the dimen-sions of his remarkable personality have become even clearer to all of us. There is no one to equal him in vigilant, warm-hearted devotion to the survivors of the Holocaust and to the sacred memory of its victims. His vitality, artistic sensibility, and imaginative generosity were in them-selves an affirmation of the Jewish will to live.
>
> We mourn him with your mother, yourself, your family and friends, and the larger family of the survivors.

After I recovered from my illness, Meni and I realized that our financial situation was in a state of chaos. We both had been unaware of Yossel's business activities. It turned out that he was highly leveraged and that his death had come at the worst possible economic moment. The prices of his various investments—art, gold, real estate—were at a low point. At the instigation of our lawyer, who wanted to settle Yossel's estate as quickly as possible, all that Yossel had worked so hard for was sold far too quickly and too cheaply. Within two years, Yossel's business instincts were validated as the value of all these assets increased dramatically. But by then, it did us no good.

The years immediately following Yossel's death were very difficult for us in every way. I moved to a smaller apartment on 68th Street and Second Avenue, less than three blocks from where Meni and Jeanie live. Meni went back to Columbia University and studied law. Jeanie was a tremendous support. But the greatest compensation occurred on January 24, 1978, when Jeanie gave birth to a little girl whom she and Meni named Joana (in Hebrew, Josefa) Deborah, after Yossel and his mother. From the beginning, everyone called her Jodi. Like most grandmothers, I love her very much, but I love her a little more because she came at a time when I needed her most. It hurts me that Yossel did not live to see her. She brought sunshine back into my life.

Meni, Jeanie, and I, wondering how we could perpetuate Yossel's name, thought of a project to document the archival material of Belsen, depicting the activities in the Belsen DP camp after the liberation and through the closing of the camp, as well as Yossel's personal documents. Nahum Goldmann and Gideon Hausner supported this plan. I worked for five years, sending many cases of materials to Yad Vashem in Jerusalem, a project that was funded by the Memorial Foundation for Jewish Culture. We decided to hand the materials over to Yad Vashem in an official ceremony in 1985, ten years after Yossel's death.

In July 1985, we went to Israel. Matthew and Nancy Mintzis, two of Meni and Jeanie's friends who had just been married, joined us as well. The formal ceremony at Yad Vashem on July 9, 1985, was chaired by Dr. Itzhak Arad, director of Yad Vashem. The auditorium was packed with personalities from Israel's political arena, friends from abroad and Israel, and above all, many *Belseners*. They had all come to pay respect to Yossel's memory.

Dr. Hausner, Jerusalem Mayor Teddy Kollek, Sam Bloch, Norbert Wollheim, and Efraim Londner all spoke movingly about Yossel. After I described my first visit to Palestine, when I came with the Jewish orphans, and the meeting I had attended on May 14, 1946, when it was first decided to establish Yad Vashem, I handed over the "Josef Rosensaft Archive of Bergen-Belsen." We were then invited to a reception at Beit Hanassi, the official residence of the President of Israel. President Chaim Herzog recalled Yossel and the first time they had met in Belsen in September 1945. I thanked him and said, "Forty years ago we were your hosts in Belsen, and we are happy that now, after reaching the highest office, you are our host."

ABOVE: Josef, Hadassah, and Menachem.Vulpera, Switzerland, summer 1953.

RIGHT: *(left to right)*
Charlie Chaplin,
Hadassah, Josef, and
Dr. Nahum Goldmann.
Vevey, Switzerland,
summer 1958.

(Photo: Eric Ed. Guignard)

LEFT: Hadassah with Brigadier H. L. Glyn Hughes. Israel, summer 1965.

(Photo: Isaac Berez)

BELOW: At the Sharon Hotel, Hadassah, seated at center, is reunited with a group of the children she had brought to Palestine from Belsen in 1946. Herzlia, Israel, summer 1958.

RIGHT: Hadassah, Josef, and Menachem with Israeli Prime Minister David Ben-Gurion. Jerusalem, June 1963.

(Photo: R. M. Kneller)

BELOW: Hadassah and Josef. San Remo, Italy, summer 1965.

ABOVE: Outside Block II at Auschwitz, with members of President Carter's Commission on the Holocaust, August 1, 1979. Hadassah is walking with *(left to right)* Sigmund Strochlitz, Commission chairman Elie Wiesel, and Mannes Schwarz.

(Photo: Interpress Photos)

LEFT: Outside Hadassah's former home at 5 Modrzejowska Street, Hadassah with Lilly and Sam Bloch. Sosnowiec, August 1, 1979.

(Photo: Jeanette Lerman)

ABOVE: Hadassah with President Ronald Reagan and a model
of the United States Holocaust Memorial Museum.
Washington, D.C.

RIGHT: Hadassah
with President Jimmy
Carter and Elie Wiesel
at the White House.
Washington, D.C.,
September 27, 1979.

LEFT: Groundbreaking of the United States Holocaust Memorial Museum, October 16, 1985. Hadassah is placing ashes from Auschwitz and Belsen on the site of the Museum, with *(left to right)* Elie Wiesel, Sigmund Strochlitz, U.S. Secretary of the Interior Donald P. Hodel, and Albert Abramson.

ABOVE: Hadassah speaking beside the Jewish Monument at a commemoration marking the 45th anniversary of the liberation. Belsen, April 22, 1990.

(Photo: John Fink)

ABOVE: Several days after Hadassah's granddaughter Jodi (Joana Deborah) was born in New York on January 24, 1978, *(from left)* Lilly and Sam Bloch; Lilly's mother, Rose Czaban; Jeanie's sister Gloria; Jeanie Rosensaft holding Jodi; David Czaban; and Hadassah.

RIGHT: Before Jodi's Bat Mitzvah, New York, January 26, 1991. Back row *(left to right)*: Lilly Bloch, Hadassah, Menachem, and Jodi. Seated *(left to right)*: Sam Bloch, David Golan, Jeanie, Gloria Bloch Golan, and Romy Golan.

ABOVE: Recalling liberation at the United States Holocaust Memorial Museum on the 50th anniversary of V-E Day. Washington, D.C., May 8, 1995.

USHMM

BELOW: Hadassah receiving honorary doctorate of humane letters from Hebrew Union College-Jewish Institute of Religion, with *(left to right)* Stanley P. Gold, chairman of the board of HUC-JIR, and Dr. Alfred P. Gottschalk, president of HUC-JIR. New York, May 25, 1995.

(Photo: Richard Lobell)

CHAPTER 18

Born in Bergen-Belsen

My son, Menachem—Meni—is a committed Jew. A Zionist, he stands up against antisemitism, all forms of injustice, fascism, neo-Nazism, and especially against the vulgarization and distortion of the history of the Holocaust. He also speaks up against any bias, discrimination, and persecution of people because of race or religion. Since his childhood, he always listened to and absorbed the survivors' stories of their bitter experiences during the Holocaust and felt compelled to write about it. One of his poems reads:

Lamentations
and even if a million dying children
did not destroy Creation
there will be another
already forgotten universe
over which God will have to cry
those tears
that should have extinguished
the fires of Auschwitz

In another poem he expresses the thought that the children of Jewish survivors have a special mission:

The Second Generation
true, we are the children
of a nocturnal twilight
the heirs of Auschwitz and Ponar
but ours is also the rainbow:
in us the storm meets sunlight
to create new colors
as we add defiant sparks
to an eternal fire

One of the reasons the ties are so strong between our children—the Second Generation, as they call themselves—and ourselves is that they grew up without grandparents, aunts and uncles, and often without siblings. They are united by the past suffering of their parents. In June 1981, at the World Gathering of Holocaust Survivors in Jerusalem, more than 1,000 sons and daughters of survivors joined their parents in an affirmation of life. At the closing session at the Western Wall, a legacy written by Elie Wiesel to be passed on to the Second Generation was read in various languages by survivors from different countries, and an acceptance, written by Meni, Jeanie, and other children of survivors, was read by members of the Second Generation. Meni read the acceptance in Yiddish.

Following this gathering, the young people formed the International Network of Children of Jewish Holocaust Survivors. Meni was elected its first chairman. The organization's leadership also included Jerzy Warman, Rositta Kenigsberg, Jeanie, Stephen Tencer (who was also born in Belsen), Eva Fogelman, Howard Butnick, Gloria Bloch Golan (Jeanie's sister), Nina Klein, Esther Fink, Joyce Celnik, and Jeanette Sieradski.

The first American Gathering of Jewish Holocaust survivors took place in Washington, D.C., in April 1983. A "Survivors Village" was constructed in the Convention Center for the event, and I was honored to open it by putting the mezuzah on the door. Jeanie was the curator of an exhibition of art by survivors entitled *The Artist as Witness*. The formal opening of the gathering took place in the huge sports arena in nearby Landover, Maryland, and was attended by more than 10,000 people. After Elie Wiesel and President Reagan had spoken, Meni came to the microphone on behalf of the Second Generation. Highlights from his speech include the following remarks:

> I was born in Bergen-Belsen. That is the essence of my being. My cradle stood only a few hundred yards from the mass graves in which Anne Frank and tens of thousands of other European Jews lie buried anonymously. My parents survived the horrors of Auschwitz; my grandparents did not. I am alive; my five-year-old brother perished in a gas chamber.
>
> We, the sons and daughters of the survivors of the Holocaust, are the bridge between two worlds. Many of us bear the names of grandparents whom we have never met. That is our heritage. For us, the Holocaust is not an abstract historical phenomenon. It is our past, our parents' lives, our grandparents' death. For us, the number six million is not merely a dispassionate statistic. It is our families, multiplied, and multiplied, and multiplied. It is my grandparents, and hundreds of thousands of Jewish grandparents. It is my parents' brothers and sisters, and millions of Jewish brothers and sisters. It is my mother's son, and more than one million Jewish children. It is shadows and echoes, nightmares and lullabies. . . . Sometimes, when I am alone, I see, or imagine that I see, the fading image of a little boy named Benjamin. Forty years ago, on Friday, April 11, 1943, that little boy was alive in the ghetto of Sosnowiec, in southern Poland. On August 4, it will be precisely 40 years since my brother was murdered by the Germans at Auschwitz. I am haunted by his face, his eyes, and I listen to a voice I never heard. But do I see him, or is it merely my own reflection? Are my tears mine, or are they his? I do not know. I shall never know. . . .
>
> We have learned from our parents' tragic experiences that the greatest crime is indifference to the suffering of others. Because of who we are, we may never be passive, or allow others to be passive, in the face of anti-semitism or any other form of racial, ethnic, or religious hatred; for we know only too well that the ultimate consequence of apathy and silence was embodied forever in the flames of Auschwitz and the mass graves of Bergen-Belsen.

From May 27 to 29, 1984, the International Network of Children of Jewish Holocaust Survivors held its first conference in New York. More than 1,600 young people from the United States and Canada participated. One of the speakers was Rabbi Dr. Isaac Levy from London, who had come to Belsen as a chaplain of the British army and officiated at the mass burial of thousands of Jews following the liberation. He recalled that one of the British officers who had heard him had said, "It was a great prayer." Rabbi Levy answered, "Forgive me, but saying kaddish over 21,000 bodies is not much of a religious act."

At the opening session of this conference at Town Hall, Meni spoke about the responsibility of the Second Generation:

> We, the sons and daughters of the survivors, have accepted the heavy responsibility inherent in our unique identity, and we have committed ourselves to providing the necessary continuity for our parents' work of the past 39 years. Together with them, we shall protect and perpetuate the sanctity and the inviolability of the memory of the Holocaust. We shall prevent it from being exploited, mythologized or desecrated by anyone for any purpose.
>
> And above all else, we shall transmit to our children our profound reverence and admiration for the spiritual strength, the heroic defiance and the somber dignity displayed throughout the years of the Holocaust by all who suffered its agonies, the victims as well as the survivors, for it is their unyielding adherence to the highest principles of Judaism and humanism which symbolizes and explains the survival of the Jewish people.

On the final day of the conference, Meni was one of the organizers of a demonstration outside the Paraguay Mission of the United Nations in New York to demand that Paraguay arrest and extradite Dr. Josef Mengele, who, the demonstrators argued, was still alive, had lived in that country under his own name, and might still be there. Elie Wiesel, Brooklyn District Attorney Elizabeth Holtzman, and Meni then delivered a petition calling for Mengele's arrest to Alfred Canete, Paraguay's Ambassador to the United Nations. Canete neither denied nor confirmed Mengele's presence in Paraguay, but stated categorically that his government was not protecting the war criminal. Meni followed up by organizing a fact-finding mission to the Paraguayan capital of Asunción to obtain information about Mengele's whereabouts. In November 1984, Meni, Holtzman, Nazi-hunter Beate Klarsfeld, and Bishop Rene Valero of the Brooklyn Archdiocese traveled to Paraguay, where they met with Justice Minister Eugene Jacquet, Interior Minister Sabino Augusto Montanaro, and President Luis Maria Argaña of Paraguay's Supreme Court. Recalling that Mengele had sent my sister and other members of our family to the gas chambers, Meni told reporter Walter Ruby, who accompanied the group to Paraguay, "For me, this search for Mengele is not just theoretical or symbolic, but very real and very personal. However, my desire to find Mengele is not a search for revenge, but rather one for justice. No one who did the things Mengele did ought to be allowed to live out his life in peace and security." Meni added, "Realistically, I do not expect to find Mengele on this trip. However, this trip, the first by an American delegation in search of Mengele . . . will put pressure on the Paraguayan government—and make clear to them how serious an issue this is in the United States."

Following that trip, there was increased interest in Mengele's fate after the war. A special U.S. Senate subcommittee came to Philadelphia in April 1985, during the third American Gathering of Holocaust Survivors, to hear testimony from witnesses who had had the misfortune of seeing Mengele every day in Birkenau in his devilish work. I was one of them. Later that year, we heard that Mengele's remains had been found in a village outside of São Paulo, Brazil. Most of the survivors did not believe this report. I shared my son's opinion when he said, "It seems too pat, too convenient."

In Philadelphia, the issue foremost on the minds of survivors, although not formally on the agenda of the gathering, was President Reagan's forthcoming visit to Germany, scheduled to coincide with the 40th anniversary of the end of World War II. In the fall of 1984, West German Chancellor Helmut Kohl, during a visit to Washington, had invited President Reagan to accompany him to a German cemetery during his next European trip, and the President had agreed. In January 1985, asked if he would consider a visit to Dachau or any other former concentration camp in Germany, Reagan said no, because such a visit would not have contributed to the theme of American-German reconciliation and friendship.

On April 11, 1985, the White House released the detailed itinerary of President Reagan's visit in Germany. Included was a stop at the military cemetery at Bitburg, in which 49 members and officers of the Waffen-SS are buried. A storm of protest came from Democrats and Republicans alike, urging the President to cancel the whole trip. Former president Richard Nixon and former secretary of state Henry Kissinger supported Reagan. Kissinger said "to back out of the visit would undermine President Reagan's credibility." To make matters worse, the President said publicly that the German soldiers buried in Bitburg cemetery "were victims, just as surely as the victims in the concentration camps." The survivors were not the only ones who were shocked. Rabbi Alexander Schindler, president of the Union of American Hebrew Congregations, in an interview in the *New York Times* on April 18, 1985, stated: "To equate the fate of members of the German army, bent on world conquest, with that of six million Jewish civilians, including one million innocent Jewish children, is a distortion of history, a perversion of language, and a callous offense to the Jewish community."

The strongest voices of protest came from Elie Wiesel and my son. In the April 16 *New York Times*, Meni was quoted as follows: "It is a tragedy that on the 40th anniversary of the liberation, we are forced to deal with the question of honoring SS men. This is morally repugnant. We are asking the President not to honor the murderers of six million Jews." On April 18, he was quoted again in the *New York Times*, stating: "The photograph of the President of the United States laying a wreath in the name of the United States at a cemetery which includes SS officers will be used and exploited by revisionist historians and neo-Nazis as proof that the President has forgiven the SS and it is now all right to forget."

On April 19, Elie Wiesel received the Congressional Gold Medal. Addressing President Reagan, Wiesel said, referring to Bitburg: "That place, Mr. President, is not your place. Your place is with the victims of the SS." On April 27, 257 members of the House of Representatives called on Chancellor Kohl to release President Reagan from his promise to visit Bitburg. In addition, 80 senators passed a resolution asking the President to reassess his itinerary, but to no avail. However, after the outcry from Jews and others, the White House announced that the President had decided to add a visit to the memorial site at Bergen-Belsen before his visit to Bitburg. This change of plans compelled Meni to declare on April 21, 1985, in his address to 5,000 survivors and children of survivors assembled in Philadelphia: "If the President insists on going to Bitburg, we do not need him and we do not want him at Bergen-Belsen. Today must be a holiday for all surviving Nazis."

Sadly, even among the leaders of the survivors there were those who were afraid of criticizing the president of the United States. Like many small-minded shtetl Jews of pre-Holocaust Europe, these individuals wanted to remain on good terms with the authorities at any cost. Months before the gathering of survivors in Philadelphia, Meni had been invited by Benjamin Meed, president of the American Gathering of Jewish Holocaust Survivors, to address the opening session in the name of the Second Generation. By the time the first day of the gathering came about, Meni had made speeches around the country attacking President Reagan for his decision to go to Bitburg. Some of the organizers of the Philadelphia gathering were uneasy about Meni's plan to attack the President in his speech. Early in the morning of April 21, Meni was summoned to a breakfast meeting. He quickly called some of the other leaders of the International Network of Children of Jewish Holocaust Survivors—Jerzy Warman, Rositta Kenigsberg, Eva Fogelman, and Michael Korenblit—and asked them to join him and Jeanie at this breakfast. There, an attempt was made to persuade Meni to limit his speech to noncontroversial topics; otherwise, he was told, he might be prevented from speaking altogether. Meni was also asked to submit a copy of his speech in advance. Meni, supported by the other members of the Second Generation as well as survivors Sam Bloch, Norbert Wollheim, and Joseph Tekulsky, rejected these demands and insisted that he would say whatever he felt he had to say.

In the end, thanks to the united front of the Second Generation leadership, the efforts to silence Meni were unsuccessful. As William Stephens wrote in the *New York Times* of April 22, "Mr. Rosensaft's speech was the most intense moment of the ceremony." It was received with thunderous applause by the thousands of survivors outside Philadelphia's Liberty Hall. That afternoon, Meni reminded me very much of Yossel.

In his Philadelphia speech, Meni said that if President Reagan's visit to Bitburg were to take place as planned, survivors and their children should demonstrate against him in Germany. "Let him pass in front of us there and look into our faces," he said, "and perhaps then, at last, he will understand the enormity of the outrage he is perpetrating." It soon became evident that the survivors would not organize or even formally participate in such a demonstration. Meni and his colleagues in the Second Generation leadership, however, were determined to do so on their own. After some discussion, they decided not to hold their protest at Bitburg but at Bergen-Belsen. A delegation was formed of 50 Americans, including children of survivors, other American Jews of the post-Holocaust generation, American war veterans who had liberated some of the concentration camps, some non-Jews, and a few Holocaust survivors. When the American authorities vetoed a peaceful protest demonstration at Belsen during the official ceremony on May 5, Meni arranged with the local German authorities that the demonstrators would be allowed to enter Belsen immediately after Reagan and Kohl's departure.

On May 4, New York Senator Daniel Patrick Moynihan devoted his nationwide radio address on behalf of the Democratic Party to the Reagan administration's treatment of the Second Generation. After explaining the background of the planned demonstration, he said:

> Two hours ago, I spoke with Mr. Rosensaft, now in Germany. He reported to me the incredible news that despite the full cooperation of the West German government, the American government has denied these American citizens the right to be present when our President is there. . . .
>
> The mind cracks, the heart breaks. What has possessed the White House?
>
> Was it not bad enough that they insisted on going through with the visit to Bitburg? That violates the right of the dead. This violates the right of the living.
>
> In the White House, two weeks ago, Elie Wiesel, a Holocaust survivor, spoke to the President and told of the ancient task of the Jews to "speak truth to power." In the most urgent, poignant but respectful manner Elie Wiesel said of Bitburg: "Mr. President, that place is not your place."
>
> Might I now say to the same president, or to any of his staff who are now listening: "Mr. President, 40 or so survivors of the Holocaust and children of survivors wish to be at Bergen-Belsen when you are there. That place, Mr. President, *is* their place."
>
> It is not only their place, Mr. President, it is their right.[11]

---

11. Senator Moynihan's radio address is reprinted in *Bitburg and Beyond,* ed. Ilya Levkov (New York: Shapolsky Books, 1987), p. 60.

On Sunday morning, May 5, shortly after President Reagan had left Belsen, 50 Jews, former inmates and children of Jewish survivors, entered the camp in a somber procession, each carrying a rose. Many were in tears. They stood around the Jewish monument and said kaddish. Then Meni spoke:

> As the son of two survivors of Auschwitz and Bergen-Belsen who suffered here and were liberated here, I speak on behalf of all the survivors and of thousands of their sons and daughters. I speak as a Jew and as an American. But above all, I speak on behalf of all those who lie buried here in these mass graves, and whose memory has now been desecrated by the President of the United States and the Chancellor of the German Federal Republic. Bergen-Belsen has today been exploited for the political interests of these men, and the sanctity of this place has been violated.
>
> Never until today has anyone dared to prevent survivors and children of survivors from standing beside these mass graves and this monument while two politicians violate their sanctity and every principle of decency by coming here on their way to honor the memory of the SS. Today the survivors of the Holocaust and their children have been deeply and permanently offended by the two politicians who failed to understand the moral imperatives of Belsen. The entire Jewish community has been insulted.

In 1987, Meni became actively involved in the deportation from the United States of another Nazi war criminal, Karl Linnas, who had been the chief of the Tartu concentration camp in Estonia in 1941 and 1942. There, he had been responsible for the mass killing of Jewish men, women, and children. In 1951, he came to the United States claiming to be a displaced person, and he had lived since then in Greenlawn, Long Island. In 1962, he was tried in absentia in the Soviet Union and sentenced to death. In 1979, Linnas was charged with having entered the United States fraudulently, and in 1981 he was stripped of his U.S. citizenship and ordered deported. However, he received support from White House director of communication Patrick Buchanan and other right-wing politicians who did not want to see anyone, even a Nazi murderer, sent to the Soviet Union.

On March 31, 1987, the *New York Times* published an article in which Meni called on U.S. Attorney General Edwin Meese III to enforce the law and sign Linnas's deportation papers. "Anything less," he wrote, "would blatantly mock justice." Instead, the Justice Department announced two weeks later, on April 15—the second day of Passover and, coincidentally, the 42nd anniversary of the liberation of Belsen—that Panama had agreed to give Linnas asylum and that he would be flying there later that day.

Meni, Elizabeth Holtzman, and Eli Rosenbaum, general counsel of the World Jewish Congress, immediately contacted the Panamanian Embassy in Washington, D.C., to protest the decision. When the Panamanian diplomats claimed to be ignorant of Linnas's Nazi past, Meni had a Washington lawyer hand-deliver copies of the legal opinions of two federal courts that set out in detail the charges against Linnas. As a result of their efforts, the Panamanian government canceled its offer of asylum to Linnas, and on April 20 he was deported to the Soviet Union for trial. Meni went to John F. Kennedy Airport to see him being brought to justice at last.

In 1988, Meni was elected national president of the Labor Zionist Alliance. Shimon Peres, at the time Israel's foreign minister and chairman of the Israel Labor Party, sent him a letter of congratulations, writing that, "I hope that you will bring American Jews who share our commitment to the fundamental principles of peace, democracy, social justice and equality into the Labor Zionist Alliance."

On December 3, 1988, Rita Hauser, chair of the American section of the International Center for Peace in the Middle East, invited Meni to join her and three other members of that organization in Stockholm to meet with Yasir Arafat, the chairman of the Palestine Liberation Organization (PLO), and other PLO leaders. The meeting was initiated by the Swedish government. The decision to accept this invitation was not an easy one for Meni, but, he explained in an article in the January 9, 1989, issue of *Newsweek,* "Would I not have wanted some American Jew in 1939 or 1940 or 1941, with or without the blessing of the American Jewish leadership, to at least try to save my brother or some other Jewish child in Nazi Europe? I did not want my daughter to someday tell me, 'You had the chance to make a difference, but you did nothing.'" He knew that he would face criticism. Still, he felt that if he did not go, he would have no right to talk about the peace process in the future. "Since I wanted others to talk to the enemy," he wrote, "I had to be willing to do so as well—not going would be a betrayal of my principles both as a Jew and as Zionist."

On December 6, the group met with Arafat and the other PLO leaders for six hours. The Swedes described the meeting as the possible beginning of a new Jewish-Palestine dialogue. One result of that meeting was a formal declaration in which the PLO for the first time publicly accepted Israel as a state in the Middle East.

The meeting was condemned by the Israel government and by many American Jewish organizations. After Meni returned to New York, there were unsuccessful efforts to oust him from a number of posts he held in Jewish and Zionist organizations, but he also received support from some Jewish leaders. Rabbi Alexander Schindler wrote to him, "Don't let the inquisitors get you down. The further from the center of power they are, the more strident they become. Those who know you, love you for following your own star, come hell or high water. In the final analysis, you have to live with yourself."

Subsequently, Meni was sharply critical of Arafat and the PLO on several occasions. In December 1989, one year after the Stockholm meeting, he published an open letter to Arafat in *Newsweek* accusing him of not living up to his Stockholm promises. "I knew, of course, that you had not overnight turned into Mother Teresa or Albert Schweitzer," Meni wrote.

> Still, you have regrettably failed to take any further substantive steps to persuade the Israeli public that their destruction has ceased to be the PLO's ultimate objective. . . . If you truly want peace, and I hope you do, you and your colleagues must do far more than you have done to date to demonstrate the sincerity of your intentions. You must renounce terrorism in fact, not merely in rhetoric. You must condemn the killing of Palestinians by Palestinians. You must encourage Palestinians to work together with Israelis for the common good of both nations. And you must allow Palestinian moderates who do not necessarily share your views to come forward without fear and join you in leading your people to peace.

After Meni's return from Stockholm, we went through a very unpleasant time. I received threatening, ugly, anonymous telephone calls, which I never mentioned to Meni. Israel eventually started meeting with Arafat and the PLO, and finally, on September 13, 1993, Israeli Prime Minister Itzhak Rabin and Yasir Arafat shook hands on the lawn of the White House. When Rabin said, "The time for peace has come," I felt that Meni had been vindicated.

CHAPTER 19

President Carter's Commission on the Holocaust

During the White House celebration of the 30th anniversary of the State of Israel in April 1978, which was attended by Prime Minister Menachem Begin, President Jimmy Carter surprised his guests by saying that the United States should have an official memorial "to the six million who were killed in the Holocaust," and announced his intention to establish a Presidential Commission to advise him on the creation of such a memorial. President Carter felt it was essential for all Americans to learn about the Holocaust and to understand its lessons because many American soldiers had participated in liberating the German concentration camps, and thousands of survivors of those camps had become American citizens.

The idea of a federal memorial to the Holocaust was conceived by Ellen Goldstein, a young woman on the staff of Stuart Eizenstat, President Carter's adviser for domestic affairs. Eizenstat endorsed Goldstein's suggestion in part because he wanted to make sure that no one in the future could deny the Holocaust. Following President Carter's announcement, Goldstein began to collect the names of potential members of a Holocaust Commission. One of the people with whom she discussed the commission was Margaret Siegel, at the time a senior official in the Department of Health, Education, and Welfare. Margie was married to Jeff Katz, one of Meni's best friends from high school and college, who was now an economist at the World Bank. Jeff had come from a highly assimilated Jewish family and used to go to synagogue with Meni and come to our Passover seders. When he and Margie were married, they asked me to be one of their witnesses.

Apparently (I found out about this only afterward), Ellen Goldstein wanted to make sure that the Holocaust Commission included at least one knowledgeable woman survivor. Margie suggested my name, and on November 1, 1978, I was formally appointed one of 34 members of the President's Commission on the Holocaust. Elie Wiesel was named chairman. There was one other survivor on the commission—Sigmund Strochlitz, from Yossel's hometown of Będzin, who, like Yossel and myself, had been liberated in Bergen-Belsen. (Sigmund's daughter Romana, who, like Meni, was born in the Bergen-Belsen DP camp, now serves with him on the U.S. Holocaust Memorial Council.) I was one of only four women on the commission—the other three were Kitty Dukakis, the wife of the then-governor of Massachusetts; historian Lucy S. Dawidowicz; and Marilyn Shubin. The commission also included former Supreme Court Justice Arthur J. Goldberg; Telford Taylor, the American prosecutor at the Nuremberg Trials; civil rights leader Bayard Rustin; Frank Lautenberg, national president of the United Jewish Appeal and later U.S. senator from New Jersey; Hyman Bookbinder of the American Jewish Committee; Senator Rudy Boschwitz from Minnesota; and the heads of the three principal Jewish theological seminaries in the United States—Dr. Gerson D. Cohen of the Jewish Theological Seminary of America (one of the rabbis who had married Meni and Jeanie), Rabbi Norman Lamm of Yeshiva University, and Dr. Alfred Gottschalk of Hebrew Union College-Jewish Institute of Religion. In due course, Fred Gottschalk became a special friend. A refugee from Nazi Germany as a child, he was one of the most important members of the commission and, later, of the U.S. Holocaust Memorial Council. He has enormous Jewish pride, a genuine understanding of history, and an absolute commitment to the mission of memorializing the victims of the Holocaust. A number of Holocaust survivors, including Thomas Buergenthal, Yaffa Eliach, Cantor Isaac Goodfriend, Miles Lerman, and Benjamin Meed, served on a 27-person advisory board to the commission.

Our assignment was to submit a report to the President "with respect to the establishment and maintenance of an appropriate memorial to those who perished in the Holocaust." It was not an easy task. We worked diligently for eight months. At the commission's first meeting in February 15, 1979, we discussed our respective visions for the contemplated memorial. On that occasion, I made the following remarks:

It is a great honor and privilege for me, a survivor of Auschwitz and Bergen-Belsen, to have been invited by the President of the United States to serve on this Commission. Ever since our liberation almost 34 years ago, we have dedicated all of our energy to keep alive the memory of the six million European Jews who perished during the Holocaust. Now, thanks to President Carter's initiative, I hope that we shall finally be able to commemorate their agony in an appropriate, dignified manner.

I hope that we shall not merely erect a memorial of stone or bronze, but that our efforts will culminate in the establishment of a major documentation center, a library consisting of all works written about the Holocaust, and significant educational projects. Our task is to create a living permanent memorial to ensure that the Holocaust will never be forgotten, or denied, or repeated.

The Holocaust was the most enormous atrocity ever committed by man against man. Henceforth, the terms "human rights," "civil rights," and "civilization" must forever reflect the background of Auschwitz, Treblinka, Bergen-Belsen, and all the other cemeteries of European Jewry. It is only proper, therefore, that there be a special day set aside each year as a national day of remembrance to commemorate the cataclysmic experience which even we, who lived through it, cannot fully comprehend. Allow me to suggest that on that day, there should be a special, nationally televised joint session of Congress dedicated to the victims of the Holocaust, and perhaps the President of the United States could deliver an annual "state of human rights" message to the country and to the world on that occasion.

Allow me also to suggest that a special national library be established, perhaps as part of the Library of Congress, in which every book that has been written and that will be written about the Holocaust, in all the different languages, will be made available to scholars, students, and those who simply want to know what happened, how it happened, and how it could have happened. This library should also serve as a means of subsidizing the publication of works about the Holocaust that otherwise would not find a publisher, or that would go out of print and become unavailable.

Furthermore, I believe that the subject of the Holocaust should be made an integral part of the curriculum of every secondary school throughout the United States. It is not enough to teach it as an elective at some universities and colleges. Rather, all children should learn what can happen when man becomes inhuman, and in this way, perhaps future generations can truly be sensitized to recognize and eliminate all forms of discrimination and persecution.

Finally, it is my deepest hope that a part of the national memorial to the Holocaust will be devoted to the one million Jewish children who perished, abandoned by the entire world. Nothing haunts me more than the memory of those frightened, hungry, tortured children. Their extermination was the most cruel, the most barbaric act in history. Symbolically, their image should be the spirit that guides our endeavors as members of this unique Commission.

Almost immediately, the principal dilemma facing us was whether the memorial would focus on the annihilation of European Jewry or would be more universal in nature. At a commission meeting on June 7, 1979, I presented my views on this important issue:

A most disturbing phenomenon has taken place in recent years. On the one hand, there are claims that the figure of 6 million is too high. Pseudo-historians intent on minimizing the impact of the Holocaust assert that the true number of Jews exterminated during the Holocaust was far smaller—4 million or 2 million. Some even deny that any Holocaust occurred. At the same time, others have attempted to enlarge the figure in order to weaken if not eliminate entirely the Jewish element of the catastrophe. These others argue that the true figure is 11 million or more.

It is true, of course, that the 6 million Jews who perished during the Holocaust were not the only casualties of World War II. However, they were the only victims of the Holocaust. And it is the purpose of this Commission to commemorate the Holocaust.

As human beings, we must remember—and mourn—all deaths,

especially those that are the result of brutality or war, those due to man's inhumanity to man. However, it is absolutely impermissible to dilute the Holocaust by categorizing it as merely another aspect of that inhumanity. The "Final Solution" was directed against the Jews, and only the Jews. No other nation was encompassed by the German genocide. Only the Gypsies were in an analogous position. And when we speak of the Holocaust, we address ourselves exclusively to the extermination of European Jewry by Nazi Germany and its active and passive international accomplices.

Allow me, as a survivor of Auschwitz and Bergen-Belsen, to emphasize again that while there were over 11 million victims of World War II, there were only 6 million victims of the Holocaust. It is distressing to me that many presumably well-intentioned academics and other commentators have failed to recognize this central dichotomy. We have said over and over since 1945 that the Holocaust was unique. Part of its uniqueness is that it was a completely separate phenomenon from the world war that took place at the same time in the same geographic locations.

The Holocaust occurred in a dimension of its own. Thus, the Jews in the Warsaw ghetto lived an existence that was unrelated to the lives of the Poles in the city outside the ghetto walls. The Jewish inmates of Auschwitz may have been in the same physical place as the Russian non-Jews who were also imprisoned there. However, they did not share the same experience. Jews were gassed as Jews, because they were Jews. The others were not. If a Russian prisoner of war was executed, he knew that it was because his nation was fighting a war with another nation. The Jews were not a part of that war. If anything, the war served as a smoke screen for the Germans to enable them to carry out their extermination of the Jews.

This Commission is a Commission on the Holocaust. Our duty is to commemorate the annihilation of the 6 million European Jews. Let us not lose sight of that objective. Of course, the Holocaust had and has major universal implications. It was not an exclusively Jewish tragedy. After all, the exterminated Jews were human beings who were murdered by other human beings. However, this universality must be distinguished from the attempt to deprive the Holocaust of its uniqueness. All other examples of mass murder must be seen in the light and shadows of the Holocaust. They may not be merged into the Holocaust.

Let us, the President's Commission on the Holocaust, therefore concentrate on our task. We are to arrive at a lasting memorial to the 6 million Jews who perished during the Holocaust in order to ensure that no such cataclysm ever occur again on this earth. That assignment, which we were given by President Carter, is monumental enough. Let us do justice to it.

The highlight of our efforts was a study mission, privately funded, to visit some of the principal sites of the Holocaust. Meni had often asked Yossel and me to take him to the towns where we were born and to the places where we had suffered during the war. We always answered, "maybe some day." In truth, neither of us thought we would ever return to Poland. I was afraid I would not have enough physical or emotional strength to revisit places that for me are filled with bitter and bittersweet memories. Still, the day came. I set out on a pilgrimage into my past, without my husband and without my son. Instead, I went as a member of the President's Commission on the Holocaust.

We were a group of 54, including members of the commission, its advisers and consultants, members of their families, and members of the commission's staff. We were to visit Poland, the Soviet Union, Denmark, and Israel. Our specific mission was to gather information before submitting our recommendations to President Carter.

We left New York on July 29, 1979. Our first stop was Warsaw. After traveling the whole night, we went directly from the airport to the Warsaw Ghetto Monument, to pay homage to the heroic Jewish fighters who had died there, alone and abandoned by the world. Looking out the window of the bus, I felt lost. I had known Warsaw well before the war, but since much of the city had been destroyed and then rebuilt, I did not recognize it. We laid a wreath at the monument, listened to Cantor Isaac Goodfriend sing El Moleh Rachamim, recited kaddish, and, with tears in our eyes, we remembered. I sensed a painful silence and emptiness. There were no more Jews in Warsaw. The streets that had once teemed with Jewishness now seemed barren. Generations of Jewish life had disappeared.

We walked—in my mind I told myself that I refused to march—accompanied by the rhythm of beating drums, to an official ceremony at the monument for the heroes of the Polish Warsaw uprising of 1944. I stood as far in the background as I could; my friend Sigmund Strochlitz asked me why. "You see," I said, "over there is the monument for the Jewish heroes of the ghetto uprising of April 1943; here is the monument for the Polish uprising of 1944. If the Poles had joined the Jews in the 1943 uprising, there would have been only one monument for all the heroes, united against a common enemy."

The following morning we went to Treblinka, passing many little towns and villages where once mostly Jews had lived but that were now *Judenrein*. At Treblinka I saw a community of ghosts, a field of stones of all sizes and shapes, each bearing the name of a city or town or village from which Jews had been brought to this place to be murdered in the gas chambers. Only one stone bears the name of an individual: "Korczak and the children," in memory of Dr. Janusz Korczak and the children of his Warsaw orphanage. Here, on an April day in 1943, members of my family—my mother's brothers, sisters, nieces, and nephews—were killed. My heart was crying as I said kaddish for them. On our way back to Warsaw no one uttered a word.

That afternoon, together with some other members of the commission, I attended a meeting of the Janusz Korczak Committee, a group of Poles, friends and disciples of Korczak, some of whom had visited him in the ghetto and had done everything in their power to save him. But Korczak had refused to abandon his children. He went with them to Treblinka and died with them there. Korczak has become a kind of folk hero in Poland, especially for Polish children. Some 104 schools are named after him, as are many children's homes and children's villages built as a fulfillment of Korczak's philosophy and dreams. The members of the Korczak Committee invited the President's Commission to work together with them on some of their projects. In Warsaw, I also attended a meeting at the Ministry of Justice at which the Minister showed us many documents and photographs depicting the Nazi crimes in the Warsaw ghetto.

On August 1, the day before Tishah b'Av, we went to Auschwitz. In our group, there were five survivors of that camp: Elie Wiesel, Sigmund Strochlitz, Mannes Schwarz, Chris Lerman, and I. As we approached the gates with their infamous inscription, *Arbeit Macht Frei,* the five of us linked arms and led the procession. We felt each other tremble as we walked on this earth drenched with blood. We saw the museum of Auschwitz and the Jewish Pavilion with its many photographs documenting the tragic truth we ourselves had witnessed. We stood in silence and grief near the crematorium where so many had been burned, laid a wreath, and said our prayers of mourning.

Then we went to Block 11, the notorious "Death Block," where Yossel had been held prisoner, naked or half-naked, for seven months, from April to November 1944. I wanted to go into the tiny cell where he had suffered so much, but the guard told me that this cell had never been opened, that there was no key. Thus, I stood outside the gate with its iron bars while Elie Wiesel spoke beautifully, movingly, about Yossel.

Outside the Death Block is the Execution Wall where many were shot and hanged. As we approached, Elie handed me a bouquet of red flowers. I placed them in silence. I wanted to say a few words, but I was choking with tears.

From Auschwitz we went to Birkenau. The five of us were still together, walking ahead of the others almost as one body. We crossed the railroad tracks that had brought us and millions of others to this place. We stopped on the site where the crematoria had once stood. Here I stood again, 36 years after I had been deported from Sosnowiec. I did not see the ruins of the chimneys or the people standing near me. I only saw myself in Birkenau in 1943. I saw our arrival, the selections, the chimneys of the crematoria spitting out tongues of fire 24 hours a day, flames that had consumed so many Jews, among them my parents, my first husband, my five-year-old son, my sister. I was standing on ashes, unable to move. Why and how did all this happen? Why did an entire world allow it to happen?

Sosnowiec is only 45 kilometers from Auschwitz. Accompanied by Lilly and Sam Bloch and by Jeanette Lerman, the daughter of Miles and Chris Lerman, I went to Sosnowiec from Auschwitz, afraid of what I would see and how I would react. New buildings have gone up and highways have been built. Otherwise, geographically and physically, the town remains the same, except in one respect: there are no Jews left. The street where I had lived is almost the same. But this street, which used to have only Jewish inhabitants, only Jewish-owned shops, except for one pharmacy, now has no Jews, not one. I stood before the house I had lived in. I looked up and saw the apartment with its balconies. Unchanged. Here I was born and raised with my brother and sister. Here I spent happy years of childhood and youth with my wonderful family. Here I was married. As I stood there, I felt I was in a strange town on a strange street in front of a strange house. Nothing was mine, perhaps it had never been mine. I left as fast as I could, never to return. I regret having returned to Sosnowiec. The dream of my childhood, of my home, is gone.

I also went to Będzin, Yossel's hometown. His house no longer stands, and the plot has been taken over by the city. We continued on to Kraków and went to the Ramu synagogue where we found a small group of local Jews, old men, many of them invalids. They looked unreal, like ghosts. We were facing the last few Jews of a once-important, culturally rich Jewish community. In Kraków, as in the rest of Poland, Hitler had won his war against the Jews.

We returned to Warsaw the same evening and the following morning flew to Kiev. At Babi Yar we saw the biggest monument ever built for victims of the Holocaust. But I am almost ashamed to admit, this monument did not move me. I was angry, and so were many others in our group. Here, the Germans had slaughtered tens of thousands of Jewish men, women, and children, but on the monument's inscription there was not one word mentioning that the victims were Jews. Elie Wiesel expressed our indignation at this falsification of history to the press as well as to the mayor of Kiev at the reception he gave for us.

From Kiev we flew to Moscow. It was my first visit to Russia, and I was looking forward to the next day, Shabbat. We all went to the synagogue to attend services. It was packed with Jewish men and women. Their beautiful prayers, chanted by their cantor and choir, still echo in my ears. It was the Shabbat of Consolation. As Elie chanted the haftarah, "Console Ye My People," we all cried. An old Russian Jew said to me, "I have never heard and I know I shall never hear again such a haftarah."

On Monday, the members of the commission divided into small groups that attended different official meetings: at the Main Archives Administration; with members of the Committee of War Veterans; at the Academy of Science (where I went); and with the Attorney General, Roman Rudenko, who had been one of the prosecutors at the Nuremberg Trials. When we reconvened after the meetings and compared notes, we realized that we had all heard virtually the same words, repeated in a dogma-like fashion by the different Russian personalities we had met. It was obvious that they totally disregarded the Jewish tragedy of the Holocaust. We were asked why we spoke about the uniqueness of *our* Holocaust; after all, they said, so many millions of others had also been killed during the war. My answer, at the meeting I attended, was that they misunderstood the reality:

> The Jewish Holocaust, our Holocaust, was not a result of the war. It began earlier, and occurred for the most part at the same time, in the same places, but it was a separate event. When Hitler came to power in 1933, he immediately began to implement his program of discrimination against the Jews, but the world ignored this. Then the Holocaust began.
>
> When in November of 1938 the Germans destroyed Jewish property, burned synagogues, and killed Jews throughout the Reich during *Kristallnacht,* the world remained indifferent. That was already the Holocaust.
>
> The war machinery only accelerated the annihilation of the Jews wherever the German boots trod. But we were not a part of the war: we were just being exterminated. We know that many others were killed during that war. We mourn them all. But our tragedy is unique—we were murdered *only* because we were Jews.

After Moscow, we flew to Copenhagen, where we were received by Danish Prime Minister Anker Jörgensen. We presented a scroll of gratitude to the Danish people for their heroic act of saving Danish Jewry during the war and another scroll to Nina Lagergren, the sister of Raoul Wallenberg, the Swedish diplomat who had saved 40,000 Hungarian Jews in Budapest at the risk of his own life. Our group's stay in Copenhagen ended with a beautiful reception at the U.S. embassy given for us by Ambassador and Mrs. Manshel.

From Copenhagen, many members of the group continued on to Israel, the last stop of our trip. We were all drained. We were met at the airport by a delegation from Yad Vashem, including Dr. Gideon Hausner and Dr. Itzhak Arad. The following day we had a series of meetings at Yad Vashem to compare thoughts.

It is significant that I, who left Poland in November 1944, when I was sent from Auschwitz to Bergen-Belsen, returned as a member of the President's Commission on the Holocaust, carrying a diplomatic passport issued by the U.S. Department of State. It was also significant that we were a diverse group of Jewish survivors and American-born Jews and Christians, young and old, black and white, all united by a common purpose. When we left the United States, we were for the most part a group of strangers. But after Warsaw and Kraków, after Auschwitz, Birkenau, and Treblinka, after Babi Yar and Moscow, after Copenhagen and Israel, we had become friends. The survivors among us had learned to appreciate the genuine empathy of those who had never before been to the places of our suffering. And they, in turn, learned about our memories, our dreams, our nightmares, our hopes. Above all, we respected one another. I am grateful to all of them. I could never have made that journey alone.

On September 27, 1979, during an official ceremony at the White House, we submitted our report to President Carter, recommending that a national Holocaust memorial museum be constructed in the nation's capital. We also recommended that there be annual national weeklong civic commemorations of the victims of the Holocaust, called "Days of Remembrance," and the establishment of a Committee on Conscience "to address contemporary instances of genocide." In his letter to the President that accompanied the report, Elie Wiesel wrote:

> Our Commission believes that because they were the principal target of Hitler's "Final Solution," we must remember the six million Jews and, through them and beyond them, but never without them, rescue from oblivion all the men, women, and children, Jewish and non-Jewish, who perished in those years in the forests and camps of the kingdom of night.
>
> The universality of the Holocaust lies in its uniqueness: the event is essentially Jewish, yet its interpretation is universal. It involved even distant nations and persons who lived far away from Birkenau's flames or who were born afterward.

President Carter praised the efforts of the commission "with my personal prayer that the memory of the Holocaust shall be transformed into a reaffirmation of life." He pledged that he would "do everything in my power to carry out the recommendations of this report. . . . And I am sure the people of this country will be looking with anticipation to this reminder of the victims and also a warning that this terrible event will never again occur on earth."

CHAPTER 20

The United States Holocaust Memorial Council

On October 7, 1980, both houses of Congress unanimously passed Public Law 96-388 establishing the United States Holocaust Memorial Council and mandating that it "construct a permanent living memorial museum to the victims of the Holocaust." I was honored to be one of the 50 Americans appointed by President Carter to serve on the Council, and to be reappointed eight years later by President Reagan. The Council was made up of Holocaust survivors, community leaders, and business executives. Among the non-Jewish members were representatives of the Polish, Ukrainian, Czech, and Slovak communities. In later years, a Roma (Gypsy), William Duna, was appointed, and rightly so. Thousands of Gypsy families were killed in the gas chambers at Birkenau. Set Momjian from Pennsylvania, an American of Armenian descent who had been a delegate to the United Nations Human Rights Commission in Geneva, was also a member of the Council. Momjian asked that the history of the 1.5 million Armenians slaughtered during World War I be included in the Museum. Although the Council at first agreed to do so, in 1991 some members insisted that the museum should focus only on events that took place during the Holocaust—that is, during the period 1933 to 1945. Momjian understood this rationale but was very unhappy about it. I supported his plea: first, because we had already voted in favor of his request a few years earlier, and second, because of Hitler's question, "Who remembers the Armenians?" I daresay that the world silence and indifference about the Armenian tragedy was a factor in giving Hitler the green light to annihilate the Jews of Europe.

Ultimately, the Executive Committee of the Council, on which I served, decided that the Armenian tragedy, because it had occurred during World War I and was not a part of the Holocaust, would not be dealt with as a separate section in the permanent exhibition, but would be included in the Archives and Library, and referred to in direct relation to the storyline of the Holocaust.

The first chairman of the U.S. Holocaust Memorial Council was Elie Wiesel. Mark Talisman, who represented the Jewish Federation, Welfare Funds, and Community Councils in Washington, D.C., was appointed vice chairman for the first term, 1980–85. Elie resigned as chairman of the Council in 1986, and President Reagan appointed Harvey Meyerhoff, a Jewish businessman from Baltimore, to be the new chairman, with William Lowenberg, a Jewish survivor of Auschwitz and a prominent San Francisco community leader, as vice chairman. In 1993, President Clinton appointed Miles Lerman, a former Jewish partisan in Poland, chairman of the Council, and Dr. Ruth Mandel, a Jewish child passenger on the *St. Louis,* vice chair. We were fortunate to have a very hard-working, committed professional staff, including Marian Craig, the liaison with Council members, who had begun working with President Carter's commission in 1979, and who became a good personal friend of mine.

I felt an awesome sense of responsibility as a member of the Council. As I told a journalist from the *Baltimore Jewish Times* in 1983, we, the survivors, are the living witnesses to the Holocaust. "We, with the numbers on our arms and the wounds in our heart, we don't need to be reminded. It is with us all the time. But we must leave memories for those who weren't there, for those who weren't born. In spite of all that has been said and all that has been written, not many people really know what happened. We must try, somehow, to let people know the truth."

We started our work by establishing various committees, including not only Council members but also others who were asked to serve and were willing to devote time and effort to help us in our work. Meni and Jeanie belonged to different committees. The full Council met only twice a year, except in emergencies. I served on the Council's Executive Committee, which met more frequently. I also chaired the Archives and Library Committee, and was fortunate to work with such capable and dedicated members of the Council staff as Elisabeth Koenig, director of the Library, and Dr. Brewster Chamberlin, head of the Archives. My first steps were to contact ambassadors from the European countries to discuss obtaining historical materials pertaining to the Holocaust from their national archives. Then

I went to Warsaw with Miles Lerman, chairman of the International Relations Committee, to enter into an agreement with the Jewish Historical Institute of Poland. We already had an agreement with the Polish Commission for the Investigation of Nazi Crimes in Poland. We went to Budapest and Prague to begin preliminary talks and later signed an agreement with Yad Vashem to work together on special projects and exchange Holocaust related archival documents.

In those years, we were able to amass 2,720,000 pages of microfilm frames plus more than one million pages of paper documents from European countries that had been occupied by Germany during the Holocaust. We also received the Vladka and Benjamin Meed "Registry of Jewish Holocaust Survivors," which lists the names and experiences of at least 65,000 Jewish survivors. Thanks to these documents, our museum will be able to teach future generations what can happen when people become inhuman. Perhaps they will be prepared to recognize and to eliminate all forms of discrimination, prejudice, and persecution.

One of the first accomplishments of the Council was its sponsorship of the International Liberators Conference, held October 26–28, 1981, at the U.S. Department of State. There, liberators met with survivors, and we heard eyewitness accounts from Allied soldiers who had liberated the camps, survivors, war correspondents, chaplains, resistance fighters, prosecutors at various war crimes tribunals, and historians. I chaired the session on medical rescue efforts. Delegations came from the United States, Belgium, Canada, Czechoslovakia, Denmark, France, Great Britain, Israel's Jewish Brigade, the Netherlands, New Zealand, Norway, Poland, Yugoslavia, and the U.S.S.R. It was an important and unforgettable event. During our session, we heard accounts by Dr. Leo Eitinger, a survivor and now professor of psychiatry at the University of Oslo; Marie K. Ellifritz, a U.S. Army nurse who had treated liberated inmates of Mauthausen; Dr. Douglas G. Kelling, who had participated in the liberation of Dachau as a medical officer in the U.S. Army; and Dr. George Tievsky, who had participated in the liberation of Dachau. They told us how those experiences had affected their lives and careers. Speaking for all the survivors of the camps, I said that the work of the doctors and nurses who had come to us with the Allied liberation armies remains a ray of light in our memory of those dark days as well, of course, as the work of our own doctors and nurses.

At the end of the session, there was an open discussion. One woman in the audience introduced herself as Ray Kaner from the Center for Holocaust Studies, a survivor of the Łódź ghetto, Auschwitz, and Bergen-Belsen. She told us how sick she had been in Bergen-Belsen and thanked me for having saved her and her friend, Sima Kaplan Heishrek. I was deeply moved but felt embarrassed when she said, addressing herself to me, that "if a person did so much good in saving others, we have to recognize this . . . . I looked for you for many years—36 years."

The Liberators Conference was a historic event that influenced the concept of the Museum. General Dwight D. Eisenhower, as Supreme Commander of the Allied Expeditionary Forces, had visited the newly liberated concentration camp Ohrdruf and on April 15, 1945, wrote to U.S. Army Chief of Staff George C. Marshall: "The things I saw beggar description. . . . The visual evidence and the verbal testimony of starvation, cruelty and bestiality were . . . overpowering. I made the visit deliberately in order to be in a position to give first hand evidence of these things if ever in the future there develops a tendency to charge these allegations merely to propaganda." These eloquent words are etched in stone on the exterior wall of the Museum.

From September 17 to 19, 1984, we held another conference at the State Department entitled "Faith in Humankind: Rescuers of Jews during the Holocaust." The major goal was to pay tribute to the righteous behavior of those good people who had the courage and conviction to hide and to save Jews, who risked their lives to help others in this time of terror and desperation. We call these people "The Righteous Among the Nations of the World"—in Hebrew, *Hasidei Umot ha-Olam*. We talked about André Trocmé and his wife, Magda, who influenced the villagers of Le Chambon to give shelter to Jews. It is estimated that 3,000 to 5,000 Jews were saved there. We talked about the Danish people who smuggled the Danish Jews to Sweden, transporting them in fishing boats. In every European country, some risked their lives to save Jews. Most were simple, unsophisticated people. What they did came from a feeling of compassion for their fellow man. We did not forget Raoul Wallenberg, the Swedish diplomat who saved 40,000 Jews in Budapest by issuing provisional Swedish passports that were honored by the German authorities. At the beginning of 1945, when the Russians liberated Hungary, Wallenberg was detained. In spite of prodigious efforts to find out what had happened to this man, we did not know then if Wallenberg died in a Soviet prison or was still alive. In order to honor the memory of this great humanitarian, we named the site of our museum "Raoul Wallenberg Place."

At the beginning of 1985, when we learned that President Reagan was planning to visit and lay a wreath at the military cemetery in Bitburg, the Council called an emergency meeting to consider resigning en masse. Our chairman, Elie Wiesel, was most eloquent in expressing our collective anger and anguish. We decided to wait, hoping that President Reagan would change his itinerary, but, as we have seen, he did not. We were also dismayed by President Reagan's comment equating the death of Nazi soldiers who fought for Hitler with the victims murdered by Hitler in the concentration camps. After President Reagan returned from Bitburg, the Council met again to discuss the possibility of submitting to the President our collective resignations. I argued against this suggestion. After all, I said, presidents come and presidents go, but our goal is to build a permanent museum to the victims of the Holocaust that will prevent future Bitburgs.

In 1992, we were invited to attend an International Conference on "Education after Auschwitz," organized by the Documentation Center in Bergen-Belsen. The Council sent a delegation consisting of Sam Bloch, Norbert Wollheim, and myself. There we met scholars, educators, and students from many countries. I was pleasantly surprised to meet young German students who were interested in studying the history of the Holocaust. They asked for advice and information. The conference took place at the same time that riots against Jews and foreigners were occurring in Germany.

One of the mandates of the Council was to establish in Washington, D.C., an annual observance of the Days of Remembrance, to encompass the internationally recognized Holocaust Remembrance Day, Yom Ha-Shoah, commemorating the six million Jews killed by the Germans during the Holocaust, and also to sponsor and encourage appropriate observances throughout the United States. A committee was made responsible for the implementation of this mandate, chaired by Sigmund Strochlitz, and later by Benjamin Meed. The first such ceremony was held on April 30, 1981, in the East Room of the White House. President Reagan participated, together with members of the Council and members of both houses of Congress. It was an unforgettable scene to see a big menorah in the White House and the lighting of six candles commemorating the six million Jews killed during the Holocaust. When I had the honor of lighting one of the candles, I was moved to tears. Here I was, a Jewish survivor of Auschwitz and Bergen-Belsen, standing in the White House next to the President of the United States, listening to a religious ceremony of remembrance.

The second National Civic Holocaust Commemoration, on April 20, 1982, was also held in the White House. This time Meni lit one of the candles. After that year, the observances of the Days of Remembrance were held in the Capitol Rotunda (except in 1988, when the Rotunda was being refurbished). Survivors, members of the Second Generation, members of the government, diplomats, and other guests are always in attendance. In addition to the speeches, candle lighting, and the reciting of the mourners' kaddish and the El Moleh Rachamim prayer, there is a dramatic presentation of the flags of the liberating U.S. Army divisions. It is always a moving experience.

In 1992, shortly before my 80th birthday, I was again invited to light one of the candles. When I arrived at the Rotunda, I learned that the President of Germany, Richard von Weizsäcker, and German Foreign Minister Genscher were sitting in the front row. I was shocked and pained. I was told that the German president was a very nice man, and I believed it, but he was sitting there not as a private, nice man, but as a representative of the country that was responsible for the Holocaust. My first impulse was to leave, but because of the solemn occasion I remained. I trembled as I lit the candle. I thought that the presence of Germans was an insult to the six million Jewish victims of the Germans.

The issue of what role, if any, the present-day German government should have in building the Museum was controversial. At one of our meetings, Miles Lerman, who headed the Development Committee, reported that some German firms and businessmen had asked to join the many Americans who had made generous mone-tary contributions to the Museum. I was very much against accepting any German money to build a Holocaust Museum, and I was glad that the majority agreed with me. The issue came up again on several occasions. A number of Council members, even including some survivors, wanted to accept funds offered by the German gov-ernment and several German foundations. Each time this subject came up, I argued that the nation that perpetrated the Holocaust, the nation of the murderers, should not contribute in any way to the memorial for their victims. With the support of other Council members, I was able to make sure that, at least while I was on the Council, no German money was accepted.

Nevertheless, the issue resurfaced several times during my time on the Council. We had to make one exception, to which I agreed as chairman of the Archives

Committee. We accepted German archives because they were essential to documenting the Holocaust.

When we were preparing the Permanent Exhibition of the Museum, Michael
Berenbaum, the Museum project director, wanted to end it with the famous photograph of West German Chancellor Willy Brandt kneeling at the monument to the
Warsaw ghetto fighters in 1970. Again, I objected and was able to keep his picture
out of the exhibition. Willy Brandt the individual was a good man, an anti-Nazi
who had left Germany in the 1930s and returned after the war in a Norwegian uniform. However, he was in Warsaw not as an individual but as the Chancellor of
West Germany. And I believe that we should not give the generation of Germans
who perpetrated the Holocaust the possibility to say that they have atoned.

CHAPTER 21

The United States Holocaust Memorial Museum

The United States government donated the land for the Holocaust Museum, which is located on one of the most prominent sites of the American capital, just off the Mall. The building itself, however, had to be constructed with privately raised funds. The Council discussed at great length whether it was to be a Jewish or an American museum. As Elie Wiesel had written in 1979 in his letter submitting the report of the President's Commission on the Holocaust to President Carter, while millions of innocent civilians were tragically killed by the Nazis and must be remembered, "there exists a moral imperative for special emphasis on the six million Jews. While not all victims were Jews, *all* Jews were victims, destined for annihilation solely because they were born Jewish." Some survivors would have preferred to have the Museum concentrate exclusively on the Jewish genocide. I disagreed strongly. The Museum was, after all, supposed to be an American national monument. As such it had to include the suffering of others. In the end, we agreed that all the victims of Nazi brutality would be remembered in the Museum, but its essence would be the Jewish tragedy.

On October 16, 1985, the groundbreaking ceremony took place. I was honored to break the ground together with the Secretary of the Interior, Donald P. Hodel. We buried six urns containing soil and ashes from Auschwitz, Treblinka, Theresienstadt, the Warsaw Jewish cemetery, and Bergen-Belsen on the site of the future Museum. That same day, we were shown a model of the museum, a five-story building to be located facing the Mall. The Museum would include a Hall of Witness, a

Permanent Exhibition, a Hall of Remembrance, with an Eternal Flame, as well as archives, a library, classrooms, auditoriums, and offices. The west front of the building was to feature a hexagonal memorial to the memory of the six million Jews killed in the Holocaust.

Over the years, the Council had several directors. Jeshajahu Weinberg served from 1989 through the building phase of the Museum. He came to us from Israel, where he had been the director of the Museum of the Diaspora. "The importance of the Museum," he said, "lies in its mission as an educational instrument. Although the Museum will have collections like other museums, the main function will be to educate through the dissemination of knowledge of the Holocaust." He worked closely with architect James Ingo Freed, a Jew who had fled Germany in 1939 with his family. A third individual who contributed a great deal to forming the Museum's identity and maintaining its integrity as a memorial to the murdered Jews of Europe was our project director, Dr. Michael Berenbaum.

One of our most important goals was to establish a memorial at the Museum dedicated to the 1.5 million Jewish children killed by the Germans during the Holocaust. This project was undertaken by the "Committee to Remember the Children," chaired by Adeline Yates, the wife of U.S. Representative Sidney Yates of Illinois. I was delegated by the Council to serve on that committee. One of the committee's most interesting programs was to develop ways of teaching the stories of the annihilated Jewish children to fourth-, fifth-, and sixth-graders in an age-appropriate way so as to avoid dwelling on the horrors and encourage them to develop sympathy for these young victims. We also wanted the Museum to have a wall dedicated to the murdered children. Schoolchildren throughout the United States were asked to paint an expression of their feelings on ceramic tiles for this wall. We received 25,000 tiles from 400 schools in 30 states, from which 3,000 tiles were chosen. I cried when I saw a tile on which an eight-year-old boy had painted two Sabbath candlesticks with two lit candles in them, underneath which he had written, "And they did not have a Sabbath."

As the building of the Museum progressed, the Content Committee, to which I belonged, came to the conclusion that although the exhibition would for the most part be chronological, certain important messages would require occasional deviations from strict chronology. We also discussed the artifacts. Over the years we had collected many historical items from abroad. The Polish government gave us a boxcar similar to those that had transported hundreds of thousands of Jews to Auschwitz, Treblinka, and the other death camps. At first, it was suggested that all visitors to the museum would have to walk through this boxcar. I objected strongly to this idea; I had already been in such a railroad car once in my life and did not want to be in one ever again, even for a few seconds. I was certain that other survivors would feel the same way. An alternate path was created around the boxcar so that visitors could choose not to go through it.

Another subject we debated was whether we should exhibit actual human hair. The Museum had received women's hair that had been shorn upon their arrival at Auschwitz. It was suggested that the hair be exhibited next to the mountains of shoes, eyeglasses, and suitcases taken from the victims. I sat through those meetings in pain, remembering how my own head had been shaved. Again, I objected vehemently. I said that hair cannot be equated with shoes or eyeglasses; it is not an object but a part of the body. It was interesting to notice that this objection came only from two female Jewish survivors—Dr. Helen Fagin and myself—perhaps because men do not feel about hair the same way women do. Men are used to shaving daily, while for a woman the shaving of her head is a violation of her womanhood.

We heard arguments that the Jewish religious law does not prohibit the public display of hair. We heard that scientists say hair is not a living tissue. But this was not the issue. It was a matter of human sensitivity. Maybe the hair that would be displayed was even mine. It should remain in Auschwitz at the place of the crime. Finally, after many discussions, the Content Committee agreed to abandon the idea of displaying the hair. I often heard it said, even by members of the Council, that this Museum was not being built for the survivors. I agree, but unfortunately it was being built *because* of the survivors and *because* of the Holocaust. Therefore, our sensitivity had to be taken into consideration.

The Museum has a very important department of oral history, videotapes of interviews with survivors of the Holocaust. I contributed to the oral history library in a small way. I always felt that the stories of the Jewish children saved and liberated in Bergen-Belsen should be told by the children themselves. Accordingly, I went to Israel in 1991 and interviewed 15 of my former children. Videotapes of these interviews are now part of the Museum's archives and library.

Finally, in April 1993, after years of hard work and planning by many who gave their time, efforts, ideas, and money with great compassion and dedication, the

United States Holocaust Memorial Museum was inaugurated. Various official events took place before the actual opening. On April 20, at the Capitol Rotunda, we observed the Days of Remembrance honoring the survivors and commemorating the 50th anniversary of the Warsaw ghetto uprising. That evening, we assembled at the Hall of Remembrance and mixed together the soil of six of the concentration and death camps and placed it under the eternal flame.

Early in the morning of April 21, we went to Arlington Cemetery to pay tribute to the American and international community of liberators and rescuers. Among the guests were American and other Allied liberators, survivors, Council members, and international delegations. A procession of honor guards took place in which each unit of the liberating armies carried the flag of its division, accompanied by a survivor. I marched with the unit carrying the British flag because I had been liberated by the British. Later I was interviewed at the Museum for the *Today Show* together with my 15-year-old granddaughter. While going through the Museum's Permanent Exhibition, I was startled to see Yossel on a video screen at a rally in Belsen in 1947, protesting against the British for sending the ship *Exodus,* filled with Jewish survivors, back from Palestine to Germany. I was shocked to see Yossel, but I am grateful that he is remembered at the Museum.

On that same day the State Department gave a luncheon, to which I was escorted by Meni. Designated Council members, international delegations, Cabinet secretaries, the Eisenhower family, and members of the Washington press corps were invited to attend. In the late afternoon, we were received at the White House. President and Mrs. Clinton greeted their guests, and President Clinton spoke about the historic significance of the opening of the museum. I felt proud and privileged to be there.

The Museum was officially opened to the public on April 22, 1993. At the dedication ceremony, held at the Eisenhower Plaza, outside the Museum, more than 3,500 people were seated and many were standing in the back even though it was a rainy, freezing-cold day. The audience consisted of Council members, survivors, members of the Second Generation, liberators, donors, members of both houses of Congress, and foreign dignitaries, including the heads of European countries occupied by the Germans during World War II. I was especially gratified that one of the speakers that day, together with President Clinton and Elie Wiesel, was President Chaim Herzog of Israel, who had been a British army officer in 1945.

Some members of the Council had objected to President Herzog's participation, arguing that only Americans should speak at the Museum's opening. However, a few of us felt strongly that the president of the Jewish state, who happened also to have served in one of the liberating Allied armies, was in a different category from other heads of state. We insisted that President Herzog had to participate in the program, and we prevailed. President Clinton, Council Chairman Harvey M. Meyerhoff, and Elie Wiesel, as founding chairman of the Council, lit the eternal flame, symbolically marking the opening of the Museum.

In the late afternoon, we dedicated the children's wall with its 3,000 tiles painted by American children. The ceremony was followed by a special program in memory of the 1.5 million Jewish children murdered by the Germans during the Holocaust. Some 400 guests heard a group of children telling the stories of their grandparents: survivors, liberators, and rescuers. One of them was my granddaughter Jodi, who began by saying, "My grandmother, Hadassah Rosensaft, has two birthdays: August 26, 1912, the day she was born, and April 15, 1945, when she was liberated from the Bergen-Belsen concentration camp."

To conclude the opening events, there was a candlelight vigil by survivors, liberators, rescuers, and family members. The following morning I went to the Museum by myself. It is far more than a memorial. It is a frightening reminder of what can happen when democratic values are destroyed by dictators and tyrants. It also stands as a warning against silence and indifference in the face of persecution and suffering. I entered the Hall of Remembrance and lit a candle in memory of my family.

CHAPTER 22

Closing Thoughts

Time passed. Meni became a successful international lawyer—as Yossel had predicted. You, my darling Jodi, grew to be a beautiful, intelligent, sensitive, and self-assured young woman. On January 26, 1991, we celebrated your becoming a Bat Mitzvah. You read your long haftarah, the Song of Deborah, magnificently. I was called to the Torah in your honor, a special experience for me. I was deeply moved that day to hear Rabbi David Lincoln, who had become a close friend of your father's, tell you in his sermon how your grandfather, my beloved Yossel, had been a hero of his when he was a boy in postwar London. And I was so very proud of you when you described in your own words how the lives and experiences of your four grandparents have affected you.

Our family became smaller and then grew again. Sadly, Lilly's parents and Sam's mother passed away. Jeanie's sister, Gloria, whom Yossel had always loved to spoil, married a young Israeli, Yoram Golan, and they have two delightful children, David and Romy.

And then came August 26, 1992. I had reached my 80th birthday! Jeanie, Meni, and Jodi gave me a beautiful dinner in their home to celebrate this milestone. They invited our family as well as a few of my friends and theirs. Among them were Meni's best friend, Robert Fagenson, now a director of the New York Stock Exchange, his wife, Margie, and their daughters, Stephanie and Jennifer. Not only have Meni and Robert remained close throughout the years, but Jeanie and Margie are also good friends. I was delighted to see this friendship continue into the next generation with Jodi, Stephanie, and Jennifer enjoying the same relationship as their parents. Also celebrating this special birthday with me were Meni and Jeanie's dear friends Sylvia and Rabbi David Posner and their children, Rachel and Raphie. Ever since Jodi and Rachel first met in nursery school, the two families have had Shabbat dinner together, alternating homes. I was also happy that my children had invited another of Meni's childhood friends, Sandra Gabrilove, now Saltzman, and her husband Michael. Sandra became a lawyer, and often comes to play canasta with me. Being with young people has always made me feel young, and this magical evening was no exception.

I still go to San Remo in the summer. I sit in the garden under a shady tree where on one side I see the blue-green Mediterranean Sea, and on the other, the swimming pool. I imagine that I see Yossel playing with our four-year-old son, holding him on his shoulders and teaching him how to swim because this ability once saved Yossel's life. I see Yossel distributing chocolate to all the children around the pool. I see him talking, joking, and playing cards with our friends. Although Yossel is gone physically, he never left me.

In 1994, as my term as a member of the U.S. Holocaust Memorial Council was approaching its end, President Clinton appointed Meni to take my place. I am proud and happy that he succeeded me, both because he is my son and also because I believe that the time has come for young people to continue our work and safeguard our legacy.

And so the days, weeks, and months pass. I see my children often. On Friday evenings, I usually get together with Sam and Lilly and their friends Helen and Abek Enisman. Abek comes from my hometown. As a young man, he worked for a dentist in Sosnowiec, and I remember him coming to my parents to buy gold for fillings. Seeing him always reminds me of my home. Once a week, I meet Lonia and three other ladies and we play cards. And of course, Jodi, I continue to derive tremendous pleasure from you. My greatest joy is listening to you telling me about your courses at Johns Hopkins, your academic interests, your friends, your singing, your new apartment in Baltimore.

In early 1995, I received a telephone call from Sara Bloomfield, the Associate Director for Public Programs at the Museum. She told me the Museum was preparing an exhibition to mark the 50th anniversary of the liberation of the concentration camps. It would show in photographs how the camps and the people looked at the moment of liberation, how they rose from ashes and returned to life. Sara asked my permission to use a comment I once made about our liberation. Of course, I agreed. When I went to see the exhibition, I read the following words of mine on a poster:

> For the greatest part of the liberated Jews, there was no ecstasy, no joy at our liberation. We had lost our families, our homes. We had no place to go, nobody to hug. Nobody was waiting for us anymore. We had been liberated from death and fear of death but not from the fear of life.

I received another telephone call in April 1995 from Jack Rodrigues, who had been one of the Dutch Jewish orphans saved and liberated in Belsen. He told me that 25 of these Dutch "children" were going to meet in Amsterdam on April 15, the night of the second Passover seder, to celebrate their liberation 50 years earlier. They invited me to join them. To my regret, I could not go, but they sent me a beautiful scroll signed by all of them, with touching remarks. I cherish this memento.

On May 8, 1995, I was invited by our Museum in Washington to speak at the commemoration of the 50th anniversary of V-E Day, the end of World War II in Europe. At the same time I was honored by the Museum with an "Award of Appreciation" in recognition of my efforts as organizer of the medical workers among the Jewish survivors of Bergen-Belsen following the liberation. Then, on May 20, 1995, Hebrew Union College-Jewish Institute of Religion in New York conferred upon me the Honorary Degree of Humane Letters in recognition of what they called my "personal commitment and moral passion" in saving Jewish orphans and bringing them "home" to Israel. I was overwhelmed by this gesture. In my acceptance speech I said: "I share this honor with all the Jewish men and women who, in spite of having been exposed to subhuman conditions in the ghettos and in the concentration camps, had the strength and the courage to help others and thereby retain their humanity."

I have had so many fulfilling events in my life and shared many years of joy with my husband and family. And yet, the ugly blue tattoo on my left arm is a constant reminder of all that not only I but also the world lost in a few short years of cruelty.

And so, my darling Jodi, this is my story. It is full of the thoughts and memories that have accumulated in my head and in my heart over all these years. It has been a blessing to watch you grow and mature. You are a wonderful person—gifted, talented, intelligent, with a wonderful sense of humor, and so very good-hearted. You have a strong Jewish identity. I pray that your generation and your descendants may be spared experiences like those we suffered, but I also want you to be aware of what can happen when people are indifferent to injustice, bias, xenophobia, the sufferings of others, and genocide.

It has not been easy for me to write this book, but always remember that I did it out of my love for you.

EPILOGUE

by Menachem Z. Rosensaft

This book was my mother's final project. She began writing it in 1994, shortly after completing her second term as a member of the United States Holocaust Memorial Council. She wrote in longhand on legal pads. When she had completed the first draft, her friend Marian Craig transcribed it for her. She then rewrote, revised, supplemented. Again, Marian lovingly transcribed the second draft. During the final year of my mother's life, as she succumbed to liver failure resulting from the malaria and hepatitis she had contracted at Birkenau, my mother spent hours on what she intended to be her legacy. When it became too difficult for her to write, she told me what she wanted changed or added.

On Friday evening, October 3, 1997, shortly after the end of Rosh Hashanah, I brought my mother a bound copy of her manuscript to the hospital. She was delighted to hold it in her hands. She was in great spirits that evening, and we spent several hours with her. And then, suddenly, she started to feel unwell, and in a matter of minutes, it was over. Jeanie, Jodi, and I were with her, holding her hand, reassuring her, and she was watching us, listening to our voices, looking at us, and then she was no longer listening, no longer hearing, no longer seeing. But she was not alone, and she did not seem to feel any pain, and she did not seem afraid.

My mother died almost exactly 22 years after my father. Her funeral was on the anniversary of my father's death. Perhaps he, who leaned on her so much, who loved her so very deeply, needed to be reunited with her. And so God allowed her to remain with us through the beginning of the New Year, to give us her blessings, to tell us that she loved us, and to hear from us how much we loved her. And then, on Friday evening between Rosh Hashanah and Yom Kippur, at the holiest moment of the year, God kissed her gently in our presence and took her to Him.

Sadly, my mother did not live to see Jodi married, but the gold ring that Mike placed on her finger under the *hupah* was one of the two wedding rings that my grandfather had made for my grandmother and my mother, and that my mother had recovered after the war. The ring is one of our family's very few heirlooms, and it was Jodi's wedding present from her grandmother and her great-grandparents.

I cannot even begin to express all that my mother meant to Jeanie, Jodi, and me. My mother always loved my poetry, and so it is in a poem that I have tried to capture the essence of her being.

Blessed Is the Soul

blessed is the soul
that lit smoke-choked darkness
from within
defying
defeating
death's shadows

blessed is the soul
that watched her own son
fade into ashes
and still sheltered
the weak
the abandoned
the sick
above all
the children

blessed is the soul
that shattered silence
confronting
frozen nocturnal eyes
at the first dawn
of reborn justice

blessed is the soul
that emerged from an abyss of bones
to create hope
not tears
to teach life
not sorrow

blessed is the soul
that left us richer
for her having been
but with an aching void
where divine sparks
will never again radiate
in the gentlest of smiles

blessed is her soul

ACKNOWLEDGMENTS

First and foremost, I am profoundly grateful to my friend and mentor, Professor Elie Wiesel, the honorary chairman of the Holocaust Survivors' Memoirs Project, for including my mother's book in the first group of memoirs to be published. As director and editor-in-chief of the project until August 2004, when I became chairman of its editorial board, I reviewed all the other submitted works, but I recused myself from making the publication decision regarding my mother's manuscript.

We are also deeply indebted to Gladys Topkis, former senior editor at Yale University Press, who edited my mother's book with tremendous sensitivity and elegance, and to Daniel and Vivian Bernstein, whose friendship helped make this second edition possible. Brewster Chamberlin, former head of the Archives of the United States Holocaust Memorial Museum, reviewed the book after my mother's death. In addition, Dr. Diane Plotkin helped my mother organize several of the book's early chapters.

—MZR
September 2005